Palgrave Studies in the History of Economic Thought

Palgrave Studies in the History of Economic Thought publishes contributions by leading scholars, illuminating key events, theories and individuals that have had a lasting impact on the development of modern-day economics. The topics covered include the development of economies, institutions and theories.

More information about this series at
http://www.palgrave.com/gp/series/14585

Aida Ramos

Shifting Capital

Mercantilism and the Economics of the Act of Union of 1707

palgrave
macmillan

Aida Ramos
University of Dallas
Irving, TX, USA

Palgrave Studies in the History of Economic Thought
ISBN 978-3-030-40364-5 ISBN 978-3-319-96403-4 (eBook)
https://doi.org/10.1007/978-3-319-96403-4

Library of Congress Control Number: 2018954336

This Palgrave Macmillan imprint is published by the registered company Springer Nature Switzerland AG
The registered company address is: Gewerbestrasse 11, 6330 Cham, Switzerland

"Some people have been of the opinion that Trade and war could not go together; but this is plainly a mistake."

—Charles Davenant, *Discourses on the Public Revenues*, 1698

Acknowledgments

I am grateful for the assistance and encouragement of many. First to my family, especially my brother Rob Ramos and my sister Rose, who encouraged me to take Seamus Deane's course on the Act of Union long ago at Notre Dame. My research as an economist has not been the same since. I am also grateful to my former advisor, also long ago at ND, Philip Mirowski, who allowed me to branch sometimes very far afield in exploring the Scottish political economy and taught me how to make hard inquiries of economic theory. The work herein is also greatly influenced by the early guidance I received on economic development from the late Drs. Denis Goulet and Roy E. Robbins, who I wish could have read it.

I am grateful to the Edinburgh University Library, Glasgow University, the University of Notre Dame Hesburgh Library, and the Scottish History Society for access to their special collections and use of their material; the King Haggar Scholars Award from the University of Dallas, which allowed me to conduct the overseas research necessary to complete this work; and my History of Economic Thought students at UD whose discussions not only sharpen my thinking, but also make me hopeful for the future. I thank those who assisted with research conversation, company, and housing, including Aaron B. Fricke, Brigid Byrne, Adena Moore, and Jeff Jasinski. I am also very grateful for the efforts of all of the staff at

Palgrave Macmillan, especially the patient Laura Pacey and Clara Heathcock. For their encouragement, incentivization, and cheer, I also wish to thank Elisa Gonzales, Patrick Gary, Kimberly Sacher, and Lt. Col. Armando Valdez.

Last but not least, I would like to thank my parents, Reynaldo and Beatrice, who have shown me the power of an enduring union.

Contents

1 Introduction 1

2 The Political and Economic Contest and Context: Scotland and England Before the Union 23

3 Beyond Trade: Mercantilist Ideas of Dependency, Value, and Transmutation and Justification of Union 43

4 Trick or Treaty: The Negotiation and Articles of Union in the Context of Mercantilist Ideas 61

5 Balancing Act: The Equivalent, Political Arithmetic, and Mercantilist Structural Violence 83

6 Shifting Capital 103

7 Unintended Consequences: Scottish Political Economy as a Reaction to Mercantilism 119

Index 139

Abbreviations

EIC	English East India Company
HMC	Historical Manuscripts Commission
L	George Lockhart's *Memoirs*
RPS	Records of the Parliament of Scotland
WN	*Wealth of Nations*

1

Introduction

Abstract This chapter discusses the importance of examining the Act of Union of 1707 as a manifestation of mercantilist economic thought. Placing the Union in the context of economic ideas sheds further light on both the contents of the treaty and the actions of the English and Scottish Parliaments. The definition of mercantilism used in the book, a system of theory and policies that seeks to maximize national power, is examined. Key aspects of English mercantilism employed in legislation before and during the negotiations—warfare without military conquest, the idea of surplus, and particular notions of wealth, power, trade, and transmutation—are introduced. How these are connected to the concept of structural violence is examined. The outline of the rest of the book is also discussed.

Keywords Act of Union, 1707 • Political economy • Mercantilism • Structural violence • Scotland • England • Eighteenth century • Imperialism • Great Britain • Power • Development

A. Ramos, *Shifting Capital*, Palgrave Studies in the History of Economic Thought,
https://doi.org/10.1007/978-3-319-96403-4_1

1.1 Economics and the Union

On May 1, 1707, a rather splendid scene unfolded, described by Sir John Clerk of Penicuik, as Queen Anne and her retinue of "at least 3 or 400 coaches," processed to St. Paul's Cathedral to celebrate the Union. Inside St. Paul's:

> The Bishops and Peers sat in galleries on her Majestie's right hand, and the late members of the House of Commons of England, with such as had been chosen to represent the Commons of Scotland in the first British Parliament, were on her left hand...[1]
>
> ...I observed a real joy and satisfaction in the citizens of London ... The whole day was spent in feastings, ringing of bells, and illuminations, and I have reason to believe at no time Scotsmen were more acceptable to the English than on this day. (1892, pp. 68–69)

Bells also rang in Edinburgh on the morning of May 1. However, rather than songs of joy, the bells of St. Giles Cathedral tolled the bittersweet tune "Why Should I Be Sad on My Wedding Day?" There were no public celebrations. Henry Maule (1707) reported to the Earl of Mar, "There is nothing so much taken notice of here today as the solemnity in the south part of Britain and the want of it here." Although the Act of Union had passed both the English and Scottish Parliaments and been ratified, the public opinion in Scotland was very much against the treaty. As evinced by the telling tune at St. Giles, Scotland had had a wedding but it was unclear whether it was to be either a happy or fruitful union.

The Act of Union of 1707 joined the parliaments and full administration of both nations into one Great Britain. For Scotland, the implications of the Act were far-reaching politically and economically. The Union not only dissolved the Scottish Parliament, and reduced the number of new ministers, but also moved the administration of the country from Edinburgh to London. As part of Great Britain, the Scottish people were subject to a new system of taxation and liable for the debt that England had accrued through the seventeenth and early eighteenth centuries. While it is undeniable that Scotland also gained economic benefits from the opening of trade with England and its overseas territories and the development of the domestic fisheries and manufacturing guaranteed by the treaty, the benefits were slow to manifest, and it is equally undeniable that the treaty also generated economic losses for Scotland in the first four decades after its passage (Whately 1989, pp. 169–176).

Public protests in print and in person both during and after the treaty negotiations showed that the public sentiment was against the Union, as analyzed in Bowie (2007) and Gibson (1988), and shown in the contemporary accounts that shall be used throughout of Scottish ministers George Lockhart (1714) and John Clerk (1993 and 1892), and English observer/propagandist Daniel Defoe (1799). There was only one public address presented to parliament in favor of the legislation.[2] And yet the majority of Scottish ministers present voted in favor of it.[3] Were the votes in favor of the Union a matter of bribery and a corruption of interests on the part of the ministers, as argued by some scholars, such as Shaw (1999), MacInnes (1990), Riley (1964), and Ferguson (1977)? Or were they a matter of confrontation of the belief that Scotland's economy could not prosper without closer alliance with England, as Smout (1969, 1964, and 1963) argues, and thus Union was the better choice than continuing to engage in commercial hostilities? Or was it simply a matter of seeing the Union as a way to secure the promises of the Revolution settlement and to secure Scotland from a return to Jacobitism? This book offers an alternative explanation of both the construction of the Union and the Scottish ministers' support for it.

The Union has been explored from a variety of viewpoints: as a fight against universal monarchy and against centrism, as a purely political exercise, as an inevitability due to geography and history (Colley 1992), as a betrayal of principle (Riley 1964; Ferguson 1977), and so on, but never yet as an exercise of mercantilism, the dominant set of economic theories of the time. The political and military reasons why the English pursued the Union are known and have been extensively explored (MacInnes 1990, 2007; Shaw 1999).[4] However less explored, especially within the economics literature, are the economic theory behind the language and actions taken as well as those called for in the time preceding the union negotiations, the drafting of the treaty, and its passage and implementation. Although the economic history of Scotland from before and during the Union has been detailed, most notably by T.C. Smout

(1963, 1964, and 1969), R.H. Campbell (1964), T.M. Devine (1985), and Christopher Whately (1989), the economic theory that underlay the Union and that guided the drafting of the articles, from the context of the history of economic thought, has not. This is a curious omission given that the dominant contemporary English economic discourse, mercantilism, is well known, and that the period that follows, the Scottish Enlightenment, led to the development of political economy as a discourse. And yet there is a dearth of material that reflects upon the influence of economic theory on the creation of the Union treaty and its passage.[5,6]

While the economic history of Scotland and the Union reports on the economic phenomena of times and places, providing rich context for discussion of policy and theory, it does not necessarily investigate the economic thinking that underlies the institutions of the times. The history of economic thought can provide a deeper analysis of both Scottish and English institutions involved, whether those institutions are formal (legislation regarding property and commerce) or informal (opinions, customs, and habits). In addition, it analyzes how those institutions are formed and unformed, and how they are changed and influenced over time or at one particular point in time. Thus, I wish to provide an analysis of the Act of Union from the perspective of the history of economic thought.

Scholarly treatments of the Union have tended to separate contemporary economic thought from analysis of the political aims of the Union's authors. An understanding of particular aspects of mercantilist thought sheds light on both the construction of the Union and the choices of its authors and negotiators. I argue that the Act of Union was created within the context of seventeenth-century English mercantilist thought that both informed and was formed by English state policy goals to remove any perceived external threats, whether military, political, or commercial, and focused on expansion through trade and the absorption of resources through colonization. Viewing the Union as merely about the expansion of trade, or the removal of the threat of a Stuart restoration and military conflict on the northern border ignores an important aspect of the intellectual history of the period, of how the prevalent economic ideas influenced the formation of policy. I do not argue that the other interpretations of the Union as a political or security measure are incorrect, but only that they are incomplete. Analyzing the actions of both the Scottish and English ministers through the lens of contemporary mercantilist thought provides additional insight into the particularities of what was perceived to be at stake, why the Union passed, and why aspects of it were so problematic to the Scottish public.[7]

I also argue that the mercantilist thought that influenced the drafting of the treaty of Union was novel in that it achieved the military and economic aims of the state without ever engaging in actual armed or commercial conflict. The relevant mercantilist theories that influenced the Union involve two forms of violence: One is psychological, the threat of violence without having to undertake either the expense or the physical action of engaging in a military invasion, and the other is structural violence, wherein the new economic and political order imposed by the Union treaty ensured that one side always had a political and economic advantage. These forms of violence are preferred to military action by a nation-state that seeks to maximize the size of its treasury, or the amount of its borrowing, because they come at lower monetary cost, but still accomplish the state's military and mercantile aims. Istvan Hont (2005) implies that to have the state act in the commercial realm was to put it into a different world of commercial affairs. What I argue instead is that mercantilism exported its economic logic and rhetoric into the political realm. Rather than seeing the state as having to commit itself to more military action, more self-defense in order to assert its commercial claims, commercial activity became a form of self-defense and a way of reinforcing the military power of states that were dominant or successful in trade because it offered not only new resources but also new avenues by which to assert their power and ability to increase their military power through the increase of physical and monetary resources available to the state treasury. Thereby it is a more efficient form of mercantilism.

The Act of Union utilizes this new mercantilism and is thus a manifestation of the mercantilist processes that the English state administration adopted in the protection and expansion of England's empire. That this is so is seen in the rhetoric and thought processes of those on both sides of the Union debate in the crafting of the Treaty, whether its progenitors were conscious of it or not. An analysis of these thought processes and language is the basis of this book, and will reveal the prevalence of the mercantilist concept of the balance, or rather a surplus that benefits one side more than another, as the dominant paradigm through which the Union was fashioned. From the perspective of mercantilist economic thinking, it can be shown that despite the benefits that were extended in the Union to Scotland, the English ministers designed the treaty such that England either broke even or, in other cases, always maintained a series of advantages, which impacted both Scotland's economic outcomes and the further development of economic theory.

1.2 Mercantilism: Growth, Power, and Violence

An exploration of the ideas of English mercantilism embedded in the Union is essential to understanding its creation and outcomes, and the reception and reaction to its outcomes. The ministers of both sides may not have always been consciously participating in mercantilist paradigms, but their actions and even the policies they voted upon were often colored by a larger mercantilist worldview. As John Maynard Keynes wrote, "The ideas of economists and philosophers, both when they are right and when they are wrong, are more powerful than is commonly understood … Practical men, who believe themselves to be quite exempt from any intellectual influences, are usually the slaves of some defunct economist" (1936, p. 383). I argue that the ideas of certain mercantilist thinkers were not only very much alive but were pivotal to the creation of the Union.

My argument focuses not on all factors of mercantilism in relation to the Union but on certain aspects of mercantilist thought and rhetoric, in McCloskey's (1998) sense of the entire set of arguments, logic, and evidence used to persuade, that were brought to bear on the crafting of the Union that have been overlooked or underemphasized in the literature. The economic aspects of the Articles of Union and its drafting have often been examined only in relation to trade. While, of course, trade is a pivotal foundation of mercantilist theory and policy, there are more complex ideas developed in mercantilist writing to justify certain actions regarding trade and politics. Adam Smith characterized the "mercantile system" in the *Wealth of Nations* (1776) as conflating wealth with specie and whose "ultimate object, however, it pretends, is always the same, to enrich the country by an advantageous balance of trade" (IV.8.1).[8] He later points to the true error of the system being its focus on production for export rather than on consumption and hence its misallocation of resources, but the criticism regarding wealth and specie persisted in the literature. While all of the economic interpretations of mercantilism have identified the common element of promoting a favorable balance of trade, the reasons given why the state should pursue such a policy tend to fall into two broad categories. Although trade and productivity is extremely important to mercantilist theory, it encompasses a more complex set of ideas than trade alone.

One line of thought follows Smith in asserting that the goal of mercantilist policy is the material betterment of the nation through the pursuit of specie gained by trade. J.R. McCulloch, Richard Jones, John Ingram, and Jacob Viner adhered to this position. The other interpretation of mercantilism sees it as a tool for building political power through economic means. The nineteenth-century German economists Gustav Schmoller, Wilhelm Roscher, and Friedrich List see the accumulation of bullion through trade as a logical means of state-building in the early national period. Eli Heckscher (1935) argues that the goal is the maximization not of the state's wealth but of the state's power. The wealth generated through mercantilist policies and practices allows the state a source of funds to consolidate and extend its power by also consolidating and extending its territory. Wealth and plenty will likely result, but in this view mercantilism uses trade and money policies to both exercise and increase its power.

Lars Magnusson (1994 and 2015) falls into the latter category but also contends that mercantilist discourse and practice reveal that wealth and power were viewed as synonymous rather than as means to an end; both are ends. Any attempt to enrich the nation is ultimately a means to bolster the state's power rather than to increase the number of goods for improved quality of life. Economic activity is manipulated to achieve the state's goals, such as restricting the trade of rival countries, and political activity is used as a means to achieve economic goals, such as the granting of official monopolies to establish control over trade routes. As Magnusson states, "Thus trade necessitated power but—at the same time power was a function of plenty and trade" (1994, p. 152). Both are expressions of state power, and the maximization of this kind of power is conceptually different than maximizing specie for funding of state unification or increased living standards. Both England and Scotland's policies in the seventeenth and eighteenth centuries fit into Magnusson's framework. For instance, England's restriction of trade for colonies and countries viewed as potential threats to its overseas dominance of trade makes sense in a worldview where maximizing trade routes is a means to international dominance. Some writers, such as William Petty, wrote to justify their own policy proposals (Hutchison 1988, pp. 29–30). Meanwhile, Charles Davenant often wrote to justify the proposals of the English government (Waddell 1958; Somers 1730). Whether the theory and policy of mercantilism is characterized as a school of thought, a rent-seeking activity (Ekelund and Tollison 1981), a set of policies, or an approach to generating solutions for specific problems (Vaggi and Groenewegen 2003, p. 16), the end goal of mercantilist writing is the same: to enact policies that maximized the wealth and power of the nation-state.

Magnusson's definition, however, underestimates the martial aspect of the favorable balance of trade/zero-sum view of exchange promoted by mercantilist policy and literature. An important sign of overseas domination is not only the expansion of territory but also the ability to grow and deploy your military overseas to defend that territory. Mercantilism is thus also an ideology of expansion through force, with international trade serving as one means to that end. Magnusson's perspective recognizes the role of power and growth through expansion in a time of expanding nation-states, and the hallmarks of national power: command over specie to fund state expenditures and control over territory and trade routes. Stern and Wennerlind's (2014) observation that the administrations of the nation-states of the period were not as organized as has perhaps previously been assumed, rather than countering the organizational features of mercantilist state policy, reinforces the need for it. The administrations of the period, whether organized or disorganized, imposed various tariffs, granted bounties, passed laws regarding labor and production regulations, and granted monopolies and privileges to private trading companies, even if they did so at the behest of competing financial and commercial domestic interests.

The balance metaphor has a long history in economic thought. As Andrea Finkelstein (2000) demonstrates, the examination in the physical sciences of the balance of forces influenced economic thinking in the seventeenth century, and was also influenced by the emergence of double-entry bookkeeping. Another influence that she claims is found in every contemporary pamphlet promoting a trade surplus is Cato's dictum, that every household should be a seller rather than a buyer (p. 91).[9] Rather than seeing a balance as maintaining a harmonious balance and exchange of equivalents as in Greek and Scholastic thought, in English mercantilist theory the emphasis is not on an even balance, but a surplus of exports or positive balance.

Salim Rashid (1993) shows that in the contemporary English literature the phrase "positive trade balance" is always used in the context of England's ongoing conflicts with France and the trade balance with that country. Wealth is thus emphasized "because the word 'wealth' carries with it connotations of both riches and power" (p. 140). Trade is discussed and understood within the framework of the politics of the period and therefore is put at the service of geopolitical power games in the seventeenth- and early eighteenth-century pamphlet literature. Thus, English mercantilist literature is crafted to advance a particular power structure of the English nation-state in relation to other states. Expansion, competition, and dominance are seen as necessary actions that maximize the power of the nation-state.

I define power as the ability to control or limit the actions of others, which definition is influenced by the work of development ethicist Denis Goulet. First outlined in *The Cruel Choice* (1971), Goulet analyzed the postcolonial realities of lesser-developed countries and the actions of developed countries that continued to prevent former colonies from exercising full agency. However, the concept applies in the seventeenth and eighteenth centuries as well. The purposeful crafting of policy in order to limit the actions of countries that one perceives a real or potential threat to the dominance of the nation-state is a mercantilist action. The goal in taking such actions is both to limit the possibility of competition and to therefore expand the dominant nation-state's potential arena for action.

On the empire of the seas, to use Armitage's (2000) phrase, to limit another country's ability to trade allows the possibility that one can seize the other's market or continue the expansion of one's market in a particular trade area.[10] To prevent a country from even being able to participate in the wider empire of the seas is an even more effective counter, as was the case with Ireland. Through this lens, the purpose of mercantilist economic policy and activity is to limit and expand certain actions in order to expand the activities of the nation-state, whether in the present or the future. It seeks to lower input costs gained at the disadvantage of its colonies and dependent territories, and to maximize the ability to expand and deploy a navy and a standing army at will, so that the actions of rivals and potential rivals seeking expansion of trade, territory, or access to physical or financial resources can be arrested.

Although it is true that the view of whether wealth was finite or infinite shifted over the course of the seventeenth and into the eighteenth century, the concept that there had to be a winner and a loser in any interaction, usually attached to the idea that resources of the world were fixed, remained in place. For emergent nation-states striving to be the winner, they could impose conditions that would ensure they were the winners. The Act of Union is one such instance of this. The mercantilist mentality provides an additional explanation of why the English used such harsh tactics to bring the Scottish ministers to the negotiating table, in the drafting of the Treaty, and why the Scottish MPs, given the imbalance of political and commercial power, had little leverage to bend the treaty to their country's fuller benefit. This explanation also provides a reason why the Scottish MPs eventually signed the treaty, despite the popular opinion against and many of their own reservations: In a mercantilist world, there was still, even after the failure of the Scottish colony at Darien, or perhaps because of it, not a way for them to become the clear winner relative to England.

The adoption of mercantilist logic was not one-sided. I argue that both the English and the Scottish negotiators used mercantilist logic and rhetoric in their arguments and proposals. A work that comes closest to the aims of this book is David Armitage's (1995) discussion of Scotland's vision of empire. Without strictly saying so, his analysis of Scotland's actions to further its economic interests in the years before the Union shows that they are working within a mercantilist paradigm. The formation of the Company of Scotland and attempts at colonization in Darien and elsewhere are the foremost examples of a mercantilist, imperialist worldview. Such mercantilist thinking is starkly present in the speeches and writing of the Scottish ministers of parliament negotiating the Union. The dominance of this framework was such that it caused other models of union to be dismissed. Andrew Fletcher's proposal for federal union and the earlier Act of Security passed by the Scottish Parliament were only acceptable if one was willing to cast aside mercantilist notions of wealth, value and valuation, and growth, and the necessity of force to attain them.

1.3 Mercantilism and Variants of Violence

Mercantilism is inherently violent due to its internal logic that one must attain a surplus or advantage over others in every interaction. Such violence has been overlooked in the literature but was apparent to contemporary writers. Adam Smith recognized the aggression and manipulation used to bring about the positive balance one desired in mercantilist thought:

> Mercantile jealousy is excited, and both inflames, and is itself inflamed, by the violence of national animosity: And the traders of both countries have announced, with all the passionate confidence of interested falsehood, the certain ruin of each, in consequence of that unfavourable balance of trade, which, they pretend, would be the infallible effect of an unrestrained commerce with the other. (WN IV.3.42)

It is a theory that in attempting to hurt the other also hinders one's own economic activity. William Paterson, founder of the Company of Scotland, opined that trade, "within the last Two Ages, it hath made greater alterations in these places of the world than the sword" (1701, p. 2).

Scottish parliamentarian and political philosopher Andrew Fletcher of Saltoun certainly saw mercantilist logic and the potential violence inherent in the Union. In *Account of a Conversation*, he discusses the possible further discouragement of Scottish trade if the Union should come to pass:

> Trade is not the only thing to be considered in the government of nations: and justice is due, even in point of trade, from one nation to another. For every good government has always encouraged industry, because all mankind have a right to the fruits of their own labor. And on that account all governments which put discouragements on the industry of their subjects are not upon a right foot; but violent, and consequently unjust. (1703, p. 418)

The Earl of Seymour replies that Fletcher speaks of injustice, "but I speak of advantage." Fletcher responds that if a nation proceeds "to take away by force any advantage that belongs to a neighboring people, you not only do injustice to them, but injure yourself by the example" (p. 429). The winner-takes-all paradigm thus instead produces two losers.

The rhetoric of mercantilism includes a language of violence, which can be political or economic. Davenant wrote, "Some people have been of the opinion that Trade and war could not go together; but this is plainly a mistake" (1698, p. 399). One can see this in the phrase "Rough Wooing" used in conjunction with English efforts to entice at different times the Scottish and the Irish to cooperate in with England's goals. Defoe's poem *Caledonia* (1706) contains the jarring conclusion that "when she's forced she's free/A perfect prostitute to industry" and that Scotland would do better to submit to English dominance and have a Union (p. 59). Even English parliamentarians concurred that the use of violence was part of the methodology of the Union process. Sir John Pakington, one of the most vocal English Tory opponents of the treaty, said the Union, "was like marrying a woman without her consent: An Union that was carried on by Corruption and Bribery within Doors, and by Force and Violence without" (in Murdoch 2008, p. 80). A non-forceful option was not offered because it is not possible in the mercantilist framework. The language of the petitions for and against Union also acknowledges this reality of mercantilist economic violence.

The violence inherent in the trade laws and hence trade patterns established by English mercantilist policy are a form of structural violence, as are some of the terms of the Articles of Union and the economic reasons that caused Scotland to enter treaty negotiations. I use the term as defined by Paul Farmer (2005) in his writing on economic development. Structural violence occurs when institutions, again whether formal as encoded in law or informal as encoded in attitudes, customs, and beliefs, are structured in such a way as to limit others' agency. In the context of the Union, structural violence is used both to force people to make choices consistent with English goals and limit the possibilities for expansion of those forced once the choices are made and policies implemented. On the whole it was a very effective means for England to expand its empire without having to engage in the expense of military conquest. Military threat prior to an economic agreement is sufficient to attain the "empire of the seas" or similarly or what amounts to the same, the "empire of commerce." The form of power manifestation in English mercantilism is not just physical but also financial. As Knights (2016) and Gauci (2001) have shown, mercantilism required the participation of a variety of players. The rise of trading companies and the subscribers who underwrote them meant that advancing a national policy by a government requires the cooperation of a network of persons outside of the formal government: merchants, financiers, and subscribers. Because merchants and subscribers have vested interests in maximizing their profit on the one hand and dividends on the other, the interests of financial mercantilism is not necessarily in the interests of the average person of the nation. The benefit to the majority of people would depend on any particular project being pursued.

The Union was merely a continuation of the maximization of English state power and deterrence of the power of other countries, and thus the violence carried over into the formation of Union as well. Structural violence is not simply a matter of rent-seeking but of purposely manipulating a situation such that another group of people are at a disadvantage. Indeed, Davenant wrote that the English should not just maximize exports over imports but that "many things must perhaps be done to thwart the interests of other nations" (1698, p. 424). Fletcher saw this too, as evidenced in the quote regarding the active removal of one party's advantage. The Treaty of Union therefore was not simply a matter of structuring governance, taxes, and trade in England's favor but also in Scotland's disfavor.

I agree with Whately (2008) that the union negotiations were more complex than a struggle between an all-powerful England and a united and poverty-stricken Scottish opposition (p. 18). I argue that both sides tended to view their situation relative to each other in mercantilist terms, and that within such a view of the world, due to its imbalance of commercial and military power, that England was able to negotiate a treaty that put itself at a structural advantage into the long term. Both used the positive balance model to assess their actions in the negotiations. The Scottish ministers focused on free trade with the colonies as their major gain. Meanwhile England had a longer-term view. Just as Thomas Mun (1664) suggested, one should view imports of resources as seeds for greater exports, England negotiated for a long-term harvest. England, more practiced in mercantilist thinking, ensured their gains in power in parliamentary representation, the location of the capital, debt service, increased tax revenue, and access to increased financial and physical capital. This is not to argue that Scotland received no economic benefits within the union framework, because it certainly did. However, it is to say that ignoring the intellectual mindset of the ministers who drafted, negotiated, and voted on the union is to overlook the strong influence of mercantilist economic thought in the shaping of Great Britain.

1.4 Shifting Capital

The Union is worthy of enduring interest and investigation. Even before the Brexit conflict or the opposition to Tory policy in the 1980s, conflicts of economic vision between groups in Scotland and England can be observed going back to 1707. The basic questions of whether Scotland should or could survive economically apart from Britain, how it would do so, whether the current situation is fair, and if a more devolved government is preferable to disunion also persist. While it may be true that sharing an island landmass may eventually cause different nation-states within it to eventually merge into one, the Act of Union as devised in

1707 was neither inevitable nor entered on equal terms. I argue that the Union, and actions taken by the English state previous to the drafting of the treaty to coerce the Scottish ministers to open negotiations, was not merely a solution for both countries to the persistent military and commercial threats each nation posed to the other, but a purposeful mercantilist measure on the part of the English state to exert economic and military power over the Scottish state. The Act of Union can be seen as a manifestation of a mercantilist economic theory that dominated English statecraft.

The purpose of the maneuverings of mercantilism and of the Union is to have control over resources and their allocation. The title of the book, *Shifting Capital*, refers to both the movement of Edinburgh's capital to London and the movement of ministers, resources, and people, or of physical, financial, and human capital, into England's command and control in manufacturing, the military, and administration. With a surplus of goods, people, and resources, the Union ensured that England emerged the winner, from a mercantilist perspective, in its engagement with Scotland, as shall be argued in the following chapters.

The movement toward Union as result of mercantilist forces began before the drafting of the Treaty. Chapter 2 explores the political and economic context of Scotland before the Union and the factors that caused them to enter the treaty negotiations. They were both at the effect of English mercantilist policies and enacted their own mercantilist countermeasures. As previously discussed by David Armitage (1995), Scotland too had encounters with mercantilist imperialist goals and with resistance to England's foreign policy interfering with their trade. The consequences of such activities and engagement with the mercantilist worldview, I argue, lead many of the Scottish ministers to see Union as the best solution and to discard alternative plans for Scotland's growth.

Chapter 3 focuses on elements of mercantilist thought and rhetoric in the works of Thomas Mun, William Petty, and Charles Davenant, pamphleteers from three different eras of English mercantilism. While there were many other voices in the mercantilist pamphlet literature, these three are a representative sample of mercantilism that focuses on the maximization of state power and that advocates doing so at the expense of other nations, even one's own allied territories. These authors were also the most widely known by the reading public and government ministers who drafted the Treaty of Union. There are different strands of thought in the works of these authors, but I focus on those regarding power, trade, defense, and dependency, and how they were put in the service of maximizing the power of the English state and minimizing the power of Ireland and Scotland. The arguments made by the pamphleteers regarding the threat and yet dependent state of Ireland is made more subtly in relation to Scotland but is replicated nevertheless in the arguments used to justify the Union. Their arguments regarding self-defense, resource allocation, and transmutation are salient to the development of the Articles of Union.

An analysis of both the arguments for Union and the Articles of Union as an exercise in mercantilism is presented in Chap. 4. Although often treated as a victory for Scotland due to free trade, it will be shown that the terms of the Treaty ensured that England would incur no losses in a mercantilist sense despite every seeming concession made to Scotland. The ways in which the logic of political arithmetic is used to confer rationality in the writing of the Articles of Union, which are sometimes very irrational in hindsight, are shown to be elements of mercantilist logic. Thus, the votes of the Scottish ministers are made more comprehensible as I argue that the majority of them are viewing the situation through a mercantilist lens. In particular, the Equivalent, the promised compensation for the inconveniences and losses of the Union, will be examined in Chap. 5 as a manifestation of mercantilist logic and political arithmetic.

If the mercantilist worldview is one in which the total wealth of the world or in any relationship is fixed and one must always seek to emerge either with an even balance or preferably to have gained from the relationship, what was it that shifted with the Union? Chapter 6 analyzes the "gains" and "losses" of both Scotland and England from the mercantilist viewpoint. In particular the movement toward security and the absorption of different forms of capital are explored in the transmutation of England and Scotland into Great Britain. The concentration of political capital in London and in the number of English parliamentarians, each a form of structural violence, ensured that Scottish interests could always be outvoted when necessary. However, the less-immediate and more immaterial gains Scotland made from the movement of its political capital and the development of its human capital paved the way for the intellectual advances of the eighteenth century.

Scottish political economy thus is made possible by and is also an answer to the conditions and causes of the Union. Chapter 7 examines the alternative to mercantilism, an unintended consequence of the Union, developed in the works of Sir James Steuart and Adam Smith. Alternative solutions for Scotland's economic problems were proposed both before and during the Union negotiations. Fletcher's proposals in particular for a federal union and the limitations of the Act of Security passed by the Scottish Parliament were one option. It was rejected however in favor of treating for union not due to a lack of viability but for a lack of compatibility with the mercantilist worldview. The outcomes of the Union, both planned and unplanned, laid the foundation for the emergence of a rejection of the mercantilist worldview in Scottish political economy. Steuart and Smith demonstrate a new vision of economic strength, value, and independence that focuses on development and growth from domestic interdependent production rather than international commercial warfare. Scottish political economy is thus both a reaction against mercantilism and an adaptation to the changes wrought by the Union.

Notes

1. Original spellings from primary sources have been preserved throughout the text in quoted material.
2. The only letter of petition in favor of the Union came from the Burgh of Montrose on October 15, 1706. Rather than an enthusiastic endorsement of the Articles however it is more a piece of economic fatalism. The "advantage of the Union," the petition says, is its elimination of the "English Prohibitory Lawes" of the Alien Act. If the laws were to be reenacted "as they undoubtedly will, we shall be deprived of the only valuable branch of our trade by which the balance is on out side and then one needs not the gift of Prophecy to fortell what shall be the fate of this poor miserable blinded nation in a few years." The Union was seen not as a liberator of trade as much as a means to prevent further damage (in Cooke and Donnachie 1998, pp. 20–21).

3. In actuality it was not the majority of all Parliamentarians but only of those present who did not abstain. The number of those who voted no, were absent, or abstained, 113, outnumbered those who voted in favor, 110, according to the signatures of the act to vote on the final draft January 16, 1707 (National Records of Scotland 1707).
4. There is also a large religious dimension to the Union debates involving the rights of the Scottish Presbyterian Kirk, which has been explored most recently in Stephen (2007).
5. Istvan Hont (2005) performs this function for contemporary political theory, mostly in relation to Andrew Fletcher, but does not apply economic theory to his analysis. He asserts that England used economics for self-preservation. I argue that political theory and economic theory codetermine each other and more than self-preservation, economic policy is used for self-expansion and aggressive limitations of others' expansion.
6. The same omission has occurred in the history of economic thought literature. While economists such as S. Todd Lowry, Tony Aspromourgos, Anthony Brewer, and Antoin Murphy have provided excellent analyses of the thought of individual mercantilists and their influence on economic policies, they have not examined how their ideas manifested in major policy such as the Union.
7. The work herein is not exhaustive of the research these issues require, but is presented as a first step toward further inquiry.
8. Citations for the *Wealth of Nations* refer to book, chapter, and paragraph number.
9. The phrase "*oportet patrem-familias vendacem esse, non emacem*," appears in Cato's *De Agricultura*.
10. Coincidentally, the main English architect of the Union treaty, John Somers (1697), stressed the idea of trade as an "empire on the sea" (pp. 1–2).

References

Armitage, D. 1995. Intellectual Origins of the Darien Venture. In *A Union for Empire*, ed. J. Robertson, 97–118. Cambridge: Cambridge University Press.

———. 2000. The Empire of the Seas, 1576–1689. In *The Ideological Origins of the British Empire*, 100–124. Cambridge: Cambridge University Press.

Bowie, K. 2007. *Scottish Public Opinion and the Anglo-Scottish Union, 1699–1707*. Suffolk: Boydell Press.

Campbell, R.H. 1964. The Anglo-Scottish Union of 1707 II, The Economic Consequences. *Economic History Review* 16: 455–477.

Clerk, J. 1892. In *Memoirs of the Life of Sir John Clerk of Penicuik*, ed. J. Gray. Edinburgh: T. and A. Constable for the Scottish History Society.

———. 1993. *History of the Union of Scotland and England*, trans. and ed. D. Duncan. Edinburgh: The Scottish History Society.

Colley, L. 1992. *Britons: Forging the Nation, 1707–1837*. New Haven: Yale.

Cooke, A., and I. Donnachie, eds. 1998. *Modern Scottish History, 1707 to the Present: Major Documents*. Edinburgh: Tuckwell Press.

Davenant, C. 1698. Discourses on the Public Revenues and on the Trade of England. In *The Political and Commercial Works*, ed. C. Whitworth, vol. 1, 127–459. London: T. Cadell, 1771.

Defoe, D. 1706. *Caledonia: A Poem in Honour of the Scots and the Scots Nation*. Edinburgh: Andrew Anderson.

———. 1799. *The History of the Union between England and Scotland*. Dublin: John Exshaw.

Devine, T.M. 1985. The Union of 1707 and Scottish Development. *Scottish Economic and Social History* 5 (1): 23–40.

Ekelund, R., and R. Tollison. 1981. *Mercantilism as a Rent-Seeking Society*. College Station: Texas A&M University Press.

Farmer, P. 2005. *Pathologies of Power*. Berkeley: University of California Press.

Ferguson, W. 1977. *Scotland's Relations with England: A Survey to 1707*. Edinburgh: The Saltire Society.

Finkelstein, A. 2000. *Harmony and the Balance: An Intellectual History of the Seventeenth Century*. Ann Arbor: University of Michigan Press.

Fletcher, A. 1703. Account of a Conversation. In *The Political Works of Andrew Fletcher of Saltoun*. London: A. Bettesworth, C. Hitch, and J. Clarke, 1732.

Gauci, P. 2001. *The Politics of Trade: The Overseas Merchant in State and Society, 1660–1720*. Oxford: Oxford University Press.

Gibson, J.S. 1988. *Playing the Scottish Card: The Franco-Jacobite Invasion of 1708*. Edinburgh: Edinburgh University Press.

Goulet, D. 1971. *The Cruel Choice: A New Concept in the Theory of Development*. New York: Atheneum.

Heckscher, E. 1935. *Mercantilism*. London: Routledge.

Hont, I. 2005. *Jealousy of Trade*. Cambridge: Belknap Press.

Hutchison, T. 1988. *Before Adam Smith*. Oxford: Basil Blackwell.

Keynes, J.M. 1936. *The General Theory of Employment, Interest, and Money*. London: Macmillan.
Knights, M. 2016. Regulation and Rival Interests in the 1690s. In *Regulating the British Economy, 1660–1850*, ed. P. Gauci, 75–93. London: Routledge.
Lockhart, G. 1714. *Memoirs Concerning the Affairs of Scotland from Queen Anne's Accession to the Throne to the Commencement of the Union*. London: Booksellers of London and Westminster.
MacInnes, A. 1990. Influencing the Vote: The Scottish Estates and the Treaty of Union of 1706–7. *History Microcomputer Review* 2: 11–25.
———. 2007. *Union and Empire: The Making of the United Kingdom in 1707*. Cambridge: Cambridge University Press.
Magnusson, L. 1994. *Mercantilism: The Shaping of an Economic Language*. London: Routledge.
———. 2015. *The Political Economy of Mercantilism*. London: Routledge.
Maule, H. 1707. Letter to the Earl of Mar, May 1, 1707, in Historical Manuscripts Commission. *Report on the Manuscripts of the Earl of Mar and Kellie Collection*. London: HMS Office, 1904, p. 389.
McCloskey, D. 1998. *The Rhetoric of Economics*. Madison: University of Wisconsin Press.
Mun, T. 1664. *England's Treasure by Forraign Trade*. London: Thomas Clark.
Murdoch, A. 2008. The Legacy of Unionism in Eighteenth-Century Scotland. In *Scotland and the Union: 1707–2007*, ed. T. Devine, 77–90. Edinburgh: Edinburgh University Press.
National Records of Scotland. 1707. *Approve of the Act Ratifying and Approving the Treaty of Union*, 16 January 1707, RH18/4/14.
Paterson, W. 1701. *Proposals & Reasons for Constituting a Council of Trade*. Edinburgh.
Rashid, S. 1993. Mercantilism as a Rent-Seeking Society? In *Mercantilist Economics*, ed. L. Magnusson, 125–142. New York: Kluwer.
Riley, P.W.J. 1964. *The English Ministers and Scotland, 1707–1727*. London: The Athlone Press.
Shaw, J.S. 1999. *The Political History of Eighteenth-Century Scotland*. London: Palgrave.
Smith, A. 1776. *An Inquiry into the Nature and Causes of the Wealth of Nations*. London: A. Millar and T. Cadell.
Smout, T.C. 1963. *Scottish Trade on the Eve of the Union*. Edinburgh: Oliver and Boyd.
———. 1964. The Anglo-Scottish Union of 1707. I. The Economic Background. *The Economic History Review* 16 (3): 455–467.

———. 1969. The Road to Union. In *Britain after the Glorious Revolution*, ed. G. Holmes, 176–196. London: Macmillan.

Somers, J. 1697. *A Letter, Balancing the Necessity of Keeping a Force in Time of Peace*. London.

———. 1730. *The True Secret History of the Lives of All the Kings and Queens of England*, 2 vols. London: D. Browne.

Stephen, J. 2007. *Scottish Presbyterians and the Act of Union of 1707*. Edinburgh: Edinburgh University Press.

Stern, P., and C. Wennerlind. 2014. *Mercantilism Reimagined*. Oxford: Oxford University Press.

Vaggi, G., and P. Groenewegen. 2003. *A Concise History of Economic Thought: From Mercantilism to Monetarism*. New York: Palgrave Macmillan.

Waddell, D. 1958. Charles Davenant (1656–1714)—A Biographical Sketch. *The Economic History Review* 11 (2): 279–288.

Whately, C. 1989. Causes and Consequences of the Union of 1707: A Survey. *Scottish Historical Review* 68 (186): 150–181.

———. 2008. *The Scots and the Union*. New York: Columbia University Press.

2

The Political and Economic Contest and Context: Scotland and England Before the Union

Abstract This chapter discusses the political and economic pressures Scotland faced that led to the creation of the Union. It focuses on issues related to trade and sovereignty. The political and economic disadvantages to Scotland's trade due to the Union of the Crowns are highlighted. The mercantilist actions and countermoves of each country are examined in the practices of the Company of Scotland in the founding of the Darien project and English attempts to thwart it. Scotland's reassertion of its sovereignty to regain control of its trade policy in the Act of Security is explained. Increasing tension between England and Scotland over control of overseas trade and the structurally violent Alien Act are explored as immediate causes of the opening of the negotiations of Union.

Keywords Union • Mercantilism • Act of Security • Alien Act • Darien • Company of Scotland • Trade • Surplus • Balance of trade • Structural violence • Union of the Crowns

A. Ramos, *Shifting Capital*, Palgrave Studies in the History of Economic Thought,
https://doi.org/10.1007/978-3-319-96403-4_2

Mercantilist thought processes dominated the formal institutional relationships between the English and the Scottish governments and their respective merchant companies before the Union. There are numerous aspects of the economic and political history of Scotland before the Union. I will focus on those relevant to England's new style of mercantilist conquest, which influenced not only trade policy but also the economic worldview of ministers of state and others. The economic and political history of the period will be analyzed from the perspective of the surplus/positive balance metaphor, the contest over various forms of capital, and the ways in which this affected the actions of policymakers, merchants, and investors of the period.

2.1 The Absent Presence: The Regal Union and English Supremacy

Part of the argument regarding the new-style mercantilism of the period is that it involves conquest without direct physical action. The first phase of this movement occurs in the first joining of England and Scotland in the Union of the Crowns. In 1603, when James VI, rightful king of both England and Scotland, moved his court to London, he became an absent monarch. The Union of the Crowns introduced the rule of Scotland at a distance, which would also be a feature of the later Union of 1707. James was also very much aware of the power of this change in Scottish politics: "Here I sit and govern it with my pen: I write and it is done; and by a Clerk of the Council I govern Scotland now, which others could not do by the sword" (quoted in Scott 1994, p. 23). The regal union was not as problematic as the Union of 1707 because the Scots still maintained a separate parliament and thus, according to their own ancient constitution, sovereignty still lay, as it ever had, with the people.

However, the regal union still brought complications. Allan MacInnes (2007) outlines three contending views of empire that were prominent through the 1650s: the Britannic, which saw Britain as the center of empire and supported incorporating union; the Scottish which emphasized republicanism and federal union; and the Gothic, which promoted the supremacy of the English Parliament in relation to the rest of Great Britain and "was exclusive in threatening to reduce Scotland (like Ireland) to a political dependency of England" (p. 54).[1] The Gothic version of Britain gained ascendancy through the Commonwealth years, when Cromwell forced a union through conquest, and the effort to incorporate Scotland into union with England did not end at the Restoration. In terms of the supremacy granted the political and trade institutions in London, Britain was being used to increase the "appropriation of Britain for England" (p. 81). The imposition of the Navigation Acts, which barred Scottish traders from commerce with the colonies and plantations, showed that the privileges being accorded to England in the regal union were not only political but also commercial, as the acts advantaged only England and not the Three Kingdoms as a whole. The Scottish sensibly made attempts for commercial union in 1664. Meetings on the proposals, spearheaded on the Scottish side by John Maitland, the Duke of Lauderdale, were not held until 1668 and ultimately yielded no results (p. 83).

While the key mercantilist engine of growth, maximizing exports, was denied to Scotland with the denial of access of trade to the colonies and plantations, other mercantilist methods were not. The Duke of Lauderdale shifted his efforts to another element of mercantilist growth, the establishment of colonies to which trade could be extended and resources and goods extracted. He was able to secure permission from the court for Scotland to engage in colonization projects in 1671. In the late 1600s, Scottish companies engaged in a number of colonization projects in the Carolinas, Nova Scotia, and East New Jersey, none of which were successful in attaining the volume of trade, or even the permanent presence of a Scottish colony, that their projectors had hoped (MacInnes 2007, pp. 164–169; Armitage 1995, pp. 99–100). Within the mercantilist framework however, given the barriers of English trade policy, there were few alternatives to these colonial projects. Thus, the eventual attempt by the Company of Scotland to build a colony and trade entrepot on the Isthmus of Panama, and the widespread support it received in Scotland, becomes more comprehensible.

2.2 Adventures in Mercantilism: The Company of Scotland and the Darien Colony

William Paterson, founder of the Bank of England and sometime monetary theorist, believed that Darien on the Isthmus of Panama would be a prime location to connect the trade of the Atlantic and the Pacific. Establishment of a colony and trading post there would boost Scotland's economic fortunes into the long run. Trade had the power to completely alter a country's fortunes, and indeed he believed it had changed history: "within the last Two Ages, it hath made greater alterations in these places of the world than the sword" (1701, p. 2). Thus, he believed trade the ultimate cure for Scotland's economic ills of monetary shortage, emigration, and low output for export: "Trade will increase trade, and money will beget money, and the trading world shall no more to want work for their hands, but will rather want hands for their work" (p. 58). He knew the country could not overtake the English East India Company (EIC), and so he decided, rather than compete with them, to circumvent them by focusing elsewhere. However, as can be seen in his *Proposals & Reasons for a Council of Trade* (1701) and *Dialogues upon the Union* (1706), despite his mercantilist outlook Paterson's goal was more the enrichment of Scotland, which was also a form of mercantilist self-defense, than the defeat of its trade rival. Given the situation of the world in regard to trade, all nations must conduct their trade and industry not only, he says, "for their advantage, but even their defence, not only for their benefit, but also of necessity" (1701, p. 3).

The Company of Scotland believed in the viability of Paterson's proposed trading colony. Just as Darien was not the first Scottish colony, other joint stock ventures preceded the Company of Scotland. Since 1617, previous trading companies included the Scottish East India and Greenland Company and the Scots Guinea Company. The former's trading rights were however suspended by James VI after protest by the English EIC and the English Muscovy Company, and the latter, although initially successful, suffered fatal losses in 1634 after its main ship was captured by the Portuguese. Other companies both for trade and for domestic improvement, like the Linen Company, continued to be established into the 1690s and there was enough capital available to support them. The condition of the Scottish economy in the late seventeenth century has been exaggerated, according to more recent accounts. Although the country had experienced two harvest failures in 1694 and 1695, which caused a loss of specie due to the need to import grain, further recessing the economy, exchange had recovered enough, bolstered by the money made available by the new Bank of Scotland. Indeed, there were at least 47 subscription-based companies established from 1690 to 1695 (Watt 2014, pp. 558–601).

In 1693, the Scottish Parliament passed the Act for Encouraging of Forraign Trade with the rationale that "nothing hath been found more effectual for the Improvement and enlargeing thereof than the Erecting and Incouraging of Companies whereby the same may be carried on by undertakings to the remotest parts, which it is not possible for single persons to undergo" (Records of the Parliament of Scotland 1693/4/107). A group of merchants founded the Company of Scotland in the same year, and were officially allowed to conduct trade overseas when the Act for the Company of Scotland Trading to Africa and the Indies was passed in 1695. Although the company invested in other projects, its major project, and the one for which it is most remembered today, was the establishment of Paterson's colony at Darien.

Originally, the Darien colony was to be a joint stock venture between English and Scottish investors. However, mercantilist logic soon exerted itself and officers of the English EIC lobbied the English Parliament to close subscriptions in England. The official arguments laid before parliament concerned the potential loss of the African and East Indies trade to the Scottish company. Their initial concern however was not necessarily the competition for trade but the competition for subscribers and the financial capital available in England. The initial subscription effort in England was very successful, raising £300,000 in ten days (*Case of Mr. William Paterson* 1708, p. 2). While the Company of Scotland did not pose an immediate threat to England's overseas trade, it did create an immediate threat to the EIC's stock price. The English subscribers to the new company were not new investors but shifted their investments from the EIC stock. From the opening of books in September 1695 to October, the English company's share price fell from £93 to £50 (Murphy 1997, pp. 70–72).

In response, the Scottish Parliament issued *A Letter from a Member of Parliament* in 1695 stating that the English would benefit from the increased competition and trade. Additionally, it made the argument that the jointly funded, Scotch-English company would "bury in oblivion, the distinguishing names of Scotch and English" (in Watt 2014, p. 823). This statement strikingly displays two relevant concepts, one mercantilist and one to do with ideas of union. The idea that shared economic categories eliminated national differences was a mercantilist idea originating in William Petty's work on Ireland wherein he categorized people by a number of different economic variables rather than by nationality, religion, or ethnicity.[2] The statement also evinces that the notion of commercial union was still alive in the Scottish mercantile consciousness. However, the English Parliament agreed with the EIC. The subscription books in London were ordered closed and impeachment was threatened for any ministers of parliament who had invested. All of the English investors withdrew their funds (Prebble 1970, pp. 51–63). After some initial success was had with subscriptions in the Netherlands and the kingdoms of Germany, the English Parliament sent letters threatening Hamburg with the king's displeasure if they continued to participate in the project, and the books were closed in both Germany and the Netherlands.

The forced closure of the books in London however only further increased the enthusiasm of the Scottish people to invest in the project. The full amount of financial capital required by the company to launch the colony was raised in Scotland. In Edinburgh, subscriptions were halted in August 1696 when £400,000 had been pledged. Support for the venture was enthusiastic and cross-sectional. John Dalrymple, the Earl of Stair (1768), describes the "frenzy of the Scots nation" that "never exceeded the rapidity with which they ran to subscribe to the Darien Company" (p. 96). Subscribers came from all parts of Scottish society, from nobility, merchants, professional guilds, lawyers, and doctors, to smaller landowners, and the royal burghs, where those of lesser means pooled their resources and invested jointly, and "young women threw their little fortunes into the stock and widows sold their jointures" to do the same. The amount raised and subscribed was not only more than the annual public revenue of Scotland but also approximately half of the available liquid capital in the country (p. 96). Because it would accept payments only in coin, bullion, and Bank of Scotland notes, a great deal of the country's financial capital was tied to the fortunes of the company (Watt 2014, p. 1601). With cash in hand, the company set about having its ships built in Amsterdam and Hamburg, as English law prohibited the use of ships built in England for uses competing with English trading interests.

The Darien venture was sound from basic contemporary mercantilist views of wealth and growth and how to attain them: through colonial expansion, resource extraction, and expansion of trade. The colony could not only produce its own goods and services for international trade, but also serve as a waypoint for exchange between the Americas and Europe, and as a source for gold and silver once mining was established. Specie could be generated for Scotland from both its mining activity and the export and reexport trade. Scotland would have an outlet for goods both to the colony and its neighbors, and a means to import goods from the New World without having to engage with English merchants and trading companies. Mercantilist trade notions were carried out with the instruments of the Financial Revolution. Funded by shareholders, the colony's subscribers would gain financial dividends. As Armitage says, the colony "was justified as a necessity in a world where the longest purse and largest population guaranteed military success, and in which the greatest empire to be captured was the empire of the seas" (p. 102). Where public debt was a means to finance commercial enterprises, undertaking overseas trade was a sensible way to attain wealth.

A combination of factors led to the colony's hardships. The climate and geography of the location of New Caledonia were unsuitable for agriculture and the first colonists suffered from extreme hunger. The Spanish were unwilling to provide aid to the colonists, likely in order to not upset their English allies in the current war, and in order to eliminate any competition for themselves in South America. A factor that could have saved the colony is if they had been allowed to trade with the plantations and colonies, but this could not be allowed by the mercantilist policy of England.

Thus, the outcome of the Darien venture was completely predictable from a mercantilist standpoint. Contending with England's mercantilist power could not work if one lacked the same relative level of military and economic strength and the capital to potentially become a strong competitor or the dominant country. The first colony failed in 1699 and the reestablished colony in 1700. There was not a basic material reason why the colony had to fail, if the colonists had been allowed relief from either English trading merchants or from an alliance with the Spanish. Both of these were blocked by English policy. The English parliament issued official proclamations to its plantations forbidding them to aid the Scottish settlers in any manner, and made an agreement with Spain that neither country would trade with the Scottish settlers (Prebble 1970, pp. 55–63). Paterson's report on the failed first colony, after the death of 200 colonists, supports this thesis:

> That their sickness and mortality happened through want of fresh provisions and strong liquors ... That the scarcity of fresh provisions and strong liquors was occasioned by the Proclamations published against them in Jamaica and the other English Plantations, which hindered several ships and brigantines that were desyned to come and others acoming to them. (1699, pp. 109–111)

When the first beleaguered colonists reached New York after sailing from Darien, they requested assistance in procuring goods, but were kept waiting for several weeks until the request was eventually refused (p. 111).

The colony was neither in itself an immediate threat to England's commercial empire, nor did it have the capability to create an immediate military threat to England or its interests. Without the military might to display and/or to enforce its power, Scotland's colony could not survive. One may well ask how the Netherlands was able to compete so well with England in the seventeenth century. The answer from the mercantilist power standpoint is that the Dutch had a developed navy, whereas Scotland had not developed its maritime power beyond the three ships of the Company of Scotland. Payments for a navy had to come from the parliament, which had a smaller pool of tax revenue to draw upon after the failure of Darien. As the time of the union grew closer, William Greg observed in a letter to English Secretary of State Robert Harley, "The great scarcity of money appears in nothing more than their recent inability to furnish provisions for a small cruising frigate appointed to guard the coast, so that the captain rather than be out of business is willing to take that in a manner upon himself" (quoted in Murphy 1997, p. 70). Why then did the English pursue the policies they did that ensured not only the beggaring of the colony but its complete demise? From a mercantilist theory of power, the policies the English pursued make more sense. In order to attain their expansionary aims, Scotland could not be allowed to have a successful mercantilist enterprise of any kind.

The collapse of the colony led to severe problems for the Company of Scotland and its investors. The loss of the financial capital that had been invested in the colony had negative implications not only for the company but also for the Scottish economy. The failure of Darien reduced the fortunes of investors and the amount of potential funds available for the Bank of Scotland. As Murphy relates, the bank had been authorized at its establishment in 1695 to hold £100,000 of capital. It began operations with only £10,000 of subscribed capital. With first the shift of funds into Darien and then a loss of those funds, there was less financial capital available for the bank's reserves. The bank's woes continued further into the early 1700s. A run on the bank occurred in December 1704, after a rumor spread that the coinage was going to be revalued, that was severe enough that it caused a suspension of business for a period of time (p. 72). Although some like John Law observed that the bank was solvent and thus there was no real monetary reason for the run to have occurred, the bank was in a precarious position due to the low level of funds available to it, which was partially a result of Darien and partially a result of the recessionary Scottish economy.

John Clerk (1993) was forthright in his assessment of Scotland's economic position after Darien:

> It was now true indeed that the Scots had become England's slaves, since they were denied not only their rights as fellow-Britons but their rights under the Law of Nations. They could not live without trade, yet were hindered from practicing it by English embargoes and their own poverty. Moreover, in the years since the union of the crowns, they had conducted their own affairs in such a way that now they could neither live in fellowship with the English nor secure their freedom by breaking away. (p. 82)

However the Scottish Parliament and merchant community had not yet given up their hopes for expansion through trade.

2.3 Countermoves: The Act of Security and the Alien Act

Further acts of English hostility aggrieved members of the Scottish Parliament and the public. The Glencoe Massacre of 1699 was believed to be the work of King William himself. Seizure of Scottish merchant ships in North America, and sometimes simply still en route to North America, continued into the 1700s. The English Act of Settlement of 1701 granted the crown to Sophia, Electress of Hanover. Although it secured the Protestant succession, the act removed 51 direct Catholic claimants to the throne. If Scotland adopted the succession, the situation created by the Union of the Crowns would endure and, of course, no Stuart monarch could ascend the throne. In 1702, England joined the War of the Spanish Succession, causing war with France, Scotland's major trading partner.

In 1703, the Scottish Parliament passed two new pieces of legislation in response to what was perceived as years of English aggression. The Act Anent Peace and War allowed Scotland to pursue its own foreign policy and the Act of Security allowed them to set aside the English succession upon the death of Queen Anne. The majority of the 1703 session consisted of debate and drafting of the Act of Security, but the entire session was of the same theme regarding the importance of Scotland's sovereignty over policy. Thus, the Parliament of 1703 bears further emphasis for its focus on the interconnection between economic and political sovereignty. Although much of the focus in the literature has been on the Act of Security and Anent Peace and War, the sessions from May to September also contained the passage of acts supporting the privileges and protections to the property and trade of the Company of Scotland, the royal burghs in relation to trade, limitations on the importation of goods from Ireland, and drawbacks on exports, and encouraging domestic wool and saltworks. Exports of English and Irish wool were prohibited. All of these are mercantilist economic growth proposals. There were also acts approved for the encouragement of economic development: the encouragement of new methods of making salt, policy for better planting of grain, and the support of new manufacturing enterprises in wool and porcelain and earthworks. An act to declare the country a free port was also presented. A commission was established to study the public revenues and whether the taxes raised during the reign of William and Mary had been used for their intended purposes. These actions demonstrate that the parliament was dedicated to undertaking economic growth on their own terms, apart from England, and in competition with it.

The Act Anent Peace and War was part of the initial deliberations in May 1703. The act declared that after the death of Queen Anne no future sovereign of Scotland could have the power to declare war without the consent of parliament, and that all treaties, including those of commerce, were left to the sovereign but required the consent of parliament. It also annulled all former legislation counter to the act (RPS 1703/5/193). Although it has been considered as a political act, separate from the economic issues that preceded it, it too is economic. The war that the English had joined in 1702 had very negative implications for Scottish trade, as did potential future conflicts that were in English interests. The power over foreign policy meant power over with whom the country was allowed to trade. Sovereignty had both political and economic implications that the Parliament of 1703 did not take lightly. A potent gesture from the parliament that was not merely symbolic was the order to publicly burn a book by James Drake that contained false statements regarding the "sovereignty and independency of this crown and nation" (RPS 1703/5/106).

Of course, Queen Anne and the English parliament refused to agree to either the Act of Security or Anent Peace and War. In an attempt to force their hand, the Scottish threatened to withhold their next contribution to the military supplies if their demands were not met. Both acts are relevant to the current discussion because both were crafted with the intention of gaining full control over Scotland's trading future. The Act Anent Peace and War was not merely about granting the Scottish Parliament power over foreign affairs. Vesting the power to declare war in parliament rather than in the monarch was a means of freeing Scotland from English foreign policy, and hence of having to sacrifice trade with her former Continental allies due to any war in which England might be engaged. Likewise, the Act of Security was about more than being able to choose the successor to the crown of Scotland.

The evolution of the Act of Security from the 1703 to the 1704 session is notable for how often the matter of trade and freedom from English interference were discussed. Queen Anne's letter opening the 1703 parliament requested money and supplies for the army for the war with France, and suggested the ministers to take up the matter of encouraging trade. In their statements to open the session, the Queen's commissioners, James Douglas, the Duke of Queensbury, and James Ogilvy, the Earl of Seafield, both also stressed the importance bolstering Scottish trade. It was John Hay, the Marquess of Tweeddale, who suggested they take up the question of the succession. All the matters were tied together however, of trade, the succession, and funding of the army. Very soon after Andrew Fletcher proposed that parliament vote that it would take any necessary action on matters regarding "our religion liberty and trade" before they would consider an act of supply for the military (Fletcher 1704, p. 35).

Fletcher pressed his compatriots to enact limitations on any sovereign who would be monarch of both England and Scotland into the next session of parliament. The Act of Security had an additional passage that was passed in 1704 that relates entirely to trade. It states that the meeting of the estates will not have the power to grant the successor to the English Crown the succession "of the Imperial Crown of this Realm" and that said successor could not be monarch of both kingdoms, "unless a free Communication of Trade, the Freedom of Navigation, and the Liberty of the Plantations be fully agreed to and established" for the subjects of Scotland by the English Parliament (in Ridpath 1704, p. 246). Debate ensued because, according to George Ridpath, some felt that the passage contained legislation they could not pass because its accomplishment depended on the actions of the English parliament. The passage was taken out of the version given to Anne for her assent, but apparently without the knowledge of all the Scottish ministers. John Clerk noted its mysterious absence in his *Memoirs* (1892, pp. 53–54).

Originally the passage was drawn from Fletcher's proposed draft for the Act of Security in which restrictions on any English succession are strongly stated. Although Fletcher's draft was rejected, the amendments to the act attempt to capture Fletcher's concerns. The passage that was voted upon replaced the Earl of Roxburgh's amendment that maintained that the successor to the English crown could not succeed to the Scottish unless he or she secured "the honour and independency" of the Scottish crown, "the freedom, frequency, and power of the Parliament, and the religion, liberty and trade of the Nation from the English or any foreign influence" (in Scott 1994, pp. 84–85). Lord Advocate Sir James Steuart was the author of the new, more specific clause:

> The same person shall in no event be capable to be King or Queen of both Kingdoms of Scotland and England unless a free communication of trade, the freedom of Navigation and the liberty of the Plantations be fully agreed and established by the Parliament and Kingdom of England in favour of the subjects and Kingdom of Scotland. (in Scott 1994, p. 85)

This was the version that was voted upon and passed in the 1704 session of parliament (RPS 1704/7/68). Given the days of discussions on the amended passage and the outcome of the vote, the majority of the Scottish parliament clearly wanted to wrest control over all the elements of their international trade back from the English court.

The English disagreed with all parts of the Act of Security, although it was granted the Royal Assent. In retaliation, in March 1705 the English passed the Alien Act, which would render any Scottish person in England an alien and his or her goods liable to forfeiture. This move threatened the Scottish merchant community the most and thus was a means both to achieve the aims of the English state through commercial force and to damage Scottish trade, and all without having to deploy a military force into Scotland. The act also denied Scotsmen in England "the liberties and privileges of Englishmen" (Lockhart 1714, p. 134). If the Scottish did not consent to meet to negotiate an incorporating union and accept the Hanoverian succession by Christmas day 1705, the Alien Act would be ratified on that day.

The English countermeasures to defeat the Company of Scotland were examples of the deployment of mercantilist policy and power abroad. Likewise, the Alien Act can be seen as another English mercantilist measure to limit the commercial, financial, and martial abilities of any Scottish person in England. Over half of Scotland's export trade was with England (Smout 1964, pp. 464–465). The community of Scottish merchants in London carried out the shipping and sale of goods from the north. Thus, the act was, as Bruce Lenman says, "a formidable economic bludgeon" (1980, p. 81). The nature of the bludgeon and its potential consequences were examined in a series of pamphlets in Scotland both for and against union. Those in support of union, such as George MacKenzie, the Earl of Cromartie (1706), the merchant Francis Grant (1707), and John Clerk (1706), argued that the already-positive balance of trade with England would simply grow stronger with joint trade policy. Those opposed to the Union, such as William Black (1706b) and Patrick Abercromby (1706), argued that the existing trade with England had hurt Scotland's own manufacturers, that the English had flooded the domestic market with their own luxury goods and did not compensate by making larger purchases of Scottish exports. Writer David Black opined, "England affords us but little of what is necessary, yet they drain us more than any nation" (1706a, p. 40). An air of frustration permeates the anti-union side, with most arguing that Scotland could instead reestablish its trade with its former Continental partners and be better off.

Besides the commercial threat of the Alien Act, the English also threatened military action. Troops were moved ever closer to the Scottish border as Christmas approached. In the meantime, the Scottish economy had already weathered a numbered of problems. Since the failure of Darien, liquidity had been an ongoing issue. The Bank of Scotland temporarily ceased payments in 1704. Being tied to England's foreign policy, as well as the loss of French trade, the continued war with France caused tariffs to be imposed on Scottish goods by France's continental allies. Threats by French pirates complicated the ventures of Scottish shipping merchants into the early 1700s. A series of crop failures resulted in severe hunger and caused a loss of specie in circulation due to the need to import large quantities of grain. The shortage of money caused a decline in other commercial transactions. The shortage had become so severe that by 1706 the Board of Trade prohibited any further movement of gold and silver out of the country. While officially Scotland was in a major recessionary period, as Whately (2008) points out, there was of course an "invisible," or, in modern terms, a "shadow economy," that was doing relatively better because its smuggler facilitators circumvented the Navigation Acts (p. 173). While the same is not true for the country as a whole, there are definite signs of pockets of the country experiencing economic growth in the early 1700s (Murphy 1997, pp. 68–70; Devine 1985, pp. 12–13). The same of course could not be said of the government, which did not have enough specie available to pay its ministers, civil service employees, or soldiers (p. 13). Given the economic issues the country faced, the martial and commercial threats engendered by the Alien Act seemed insurmountable.

This was however the point of having enacted the Alien Act. Rather than a simple countermove to the Act of Security, the Alien Act was a deliberate attempt to force the Scots into an incorporating union. Baron John Somers[3] (1730), who was to shortly play a major role in the drafting of the Articles of Union, writes of the machinations of the period and sheds light on how it was that the Act of Security gained the Royal Assent when it required some English Parliamentary agreement: "it seemd to have been a deep and secret act of policy in our Ministry, to let them have their Act of Security, that they might be brought into a greater dilemma than before, and be obliged to come to our terms; and so it prov'd" (p. 283). According to Somers, Lord Treasurer Sidney Godolphin, later a commissioner of the Union, had approved the Act of Security with the idea of the Alien Act already in mind, and the ultimate goal of course was the maximization of English power that the endgame of an incorporating union would bring. William Greg reported to English Secretary of State Robert Harley: "They begin to be sensible of the great loss they will be at after the 25th of December when they shall see their small incomes curtailed of 80,000 pds., which their black cattle and linen cloth brought them yearly from England" (quoted in Murphy 1997, pp. 69–70).

Meanwhile, tensions escalated between Scottish and English shipping merchants. In the spring of 1704, the Company of Scotland seized the English ship *Worcester* and tried its captain and two crewmen (*Darien Shipping Papers* 1924, p. xv). The warrant for the men's arrest is unapologetic in stating that these actions were taken in retaliation for the English seizure of a Scottish ship in London and only after considering:

> the repeated Injurious Acts of Violence, Oppression, injustice and indignity committed ... by the English East India Company and their Adherents; particularly in what they have done concerning the Ship *Annandale*, contrary to the Law of Nations, and to the Municipal Laws of both kingdoms; And that all friendly methods hitherto used for obtaining reparation thereof have proved ineffectuall... (Company of Scotland 1704, "Warrant...," p. 263)

The Scottish Court of Admiralty found the captain and crew guilty of piracy. This matter did nothing to allay the animosity between the contending parties.

The Scottish Parliament that met in June 1705 still sought alternatives to their situation. The first order of business in the session of June 28 concerned trade. George Lockhart did not discuss all of the proposals considered and passed, as he thought it was bad practice to delay discussion of the treaty in order to discuss trade. However, the session records show an assertion of mercantilist economic power against England. Acts were passed to prohibit the importation of English butter and cheese, the encouragement of the fishing trade, the duty-free exportation of beef and pork and wool, and the establishment of a Council of Trade (RPS 1705/6/191). The council was formally established, Lockhart says, "with power to put the laws in relation to trade in execution" and balance the trade deficit. He deemed this measure "very necessary; for the merchants met with no encouragement, and trade was carried on without any regards to the methods prescribed by law, and the interest of the nation" (p. 144). Proposals by John Law and Hugh Chamberlen for the establishment of a land bank that would increase the liquidity of the country by allowing the gentry to open accounts based on the value of their land, were considered but rejected.[4] Law's proposed land bank would have alleviated the shortage of coin being experienced throughout the country, and was an alternative to the dominant mercantilist monetary theory that more money could be had only by exporting more than one imported. The remainder of the parliamentary session was spent discussing the advantages and disadvantages of union. Because of the combination of pressures on Scotland's economy from both within and without, the majority present voted for treaty negotiations to begin in 1706. The Alien Act was rescinded and Queen Anne appointed commissioners from both sides to draft the treaty (Murphy 1997, pp. 68–70).

Despite the hopefulness of many in the Scottish Parliament regarding the negotiations, David Black issued a warning in his pamphlet that pressed Scotland to care for its interests because: "the English know better how to manage their interest; and altho' they have rescinded their Act declaring us Alien, yet both before and since passing that Act, they effectually make us so, and if we do not look to our selves, in a short time they will sink us"

(p. 31). Given some aspects of the treaty negotiations and the gains and losses of each side in the final Articles, Black's warning was prescient.

While it may have seemed that the negotiations for the Treaty of Union was a cessation of the mercantilist contest between the two nations, it was merely the continuation of it, albeit in a different form, as shall be demonstrated in Chaps. 4, 5, and 6 after a deeper discussion of relevant mercantilist theories, beyond the concepts of positive balance and maximization of power, in Chap. 3.

Notes

1. For legal and other issues surrounding the Union of the Crowns and Scottish sovereignty that impacted the discourse in 1707, see W. Ferguson (1974).
2. This concept in Petty's work is explored in greater detail in Chap. 3.
3. Also variously spelled "Sommers" in some writings. However, his signature on the final copy of the Articles of Union has only one "m."
4. Murphy addresses the potential issue that the Country party may have had with Law's proposed Land Bank. Since King William's closing of the Darien subscriptions in London, the directors of the Bank of Scotland had lent their support to the Stuart restoration. Thus, the supporters of the Hanoverian succession in the Court party and the Squadrone Volante welcomed a possible rival to the Bank (70). That they supported it on those grounds shows mercantilist thinking, that a new bank would limit the activity of the Bank of Scotland, rather than what law was actually proposing: a means of relieving Scotland's coinage crisis by increasing the money in circulation.

References

Abercromby, P. 1706. *The Advantages of the Act of Security, Compar'd with these of the Intended Union*. Edinburgh.

Armitage, David. 1995. Intellectual Origins of the Darien Venture. In *A Union for Empire*, ed. J. Robertson, 97–118. Cambridge: Cambridge University Press.

Black, D. 1706. *An Essay Upon Industry and Trade*. Edinburgh: James Watson.

Black, W. 1706. *Answer to a Letter Concerning Trade*. Edinburgh.
The Case of Mr. William Paterson in Relation to His Claim on the Equivalent. 1708. Edinburgh.
Clerk, J. 1706. *A Letter to a Friend, Giving an Account How the Treaty of Union Has Been Received Here*. Edinburgh.
———. 1892. *Memoirs of the Life of Sir John Clerk of Pennicuik*, ed. J. Gray. Edinburgh: T. and A. Constable for the Scottish History Society.
———. 1993. *History of the Union of Scotland and England*, trans. and ed. D. Duncan. Edinburgh: The Scottish History Society.
Company of Scotland. 1704. Warrant for the Capture of the East India Ship 'Worcester'. In *Darien Shipping Papers*, ed. G.P. Insh. Edinburgh: Edinburgh University Press for the Scottish History Society, 1924.
Dalrymple, J. 1768. *Memoirs of Great Britain and Ireland*. Vol. 2. Edinburgh: J. Bell and W. Creech.
Devine, T.M. 1985. The Union of 1707 and Scottish Development. *Scottish Economic and Social History* 5 (28): 23–40.
Ferguson, W. 1974. Imperial Crowns: A Neglected Facet of the Background of the Treaty of Union of 1707. *Scottish Historical Review* 53 (155): 22–44.
Grant, F. 1707. *The Patriot Resolved*. Edinburgh.
Lenman, B. 1980. *The Jacobite Risings in Britain, 1689–1746*. Edinburgh: Holmes and Meier.
A Letter from a Member of Parliament to his Friend in the Country. 1704. London: Booksellers of London and Westminster.
Lockhart, G. 1714. *Memoirs Concerning the Affairs of Scotland from Queen Anne's Accession to the Throne to the Commencement of the Union*. London: Booksellers of London and Westminster.
MacInnes, A. 2007. *Union and Empire: The Making of the United Kingdom in 1707*. Cambridge: Cambridge University Press.
MacKenzie, G. 1706. *A Letter from the Earl of Cromartie to the Earl of Wharton Concerning the Union*. Edinburgh.
Murphy, A. 1997. *John Law: Economic Theorist and Policy-Maker*. Oxford: The Clarendon Press.
Paterson, W. 1699. Report of Matters Relating to the Colony of Caledonia. In *Darien Shipping Papers*, ed. G.P. Insh. Edinburgh: University Press for the Scottish History Society, 1924.
———. 1701. *Proposals & Reasons for Constituting a Council of Trade*. Edinburgh.
———. 1706. Dialogues Upon the Union. In *The Writings of William Paterson*, ed. S. Bannister, 163–251. London: Effingham Wilson, 1858.

Prebble, J. 1970. *The Darien Disaster*. Harmondsworth, UK: Penguin Books.

Records of the Parliament of Scotland to 1707. 1693–1705. Ed. K.M. Brown, et al. St. Andrews 2007–2018, available at http://www.rps.ac.uk/trans. Accessed 18 June 2018.

Ridpath, G. 1704. *An Account of the Proceedings of the Parliament of Scotland, Which Met at Edinburgh, May 6, 1703*. Edinburgh.

Scott, P.H. 1994. *Andrew Fletcher and the Act of Union*. Edinburgh: The Saltire Society.

Smout, T.C. 1964. The Anglo-Scottish Union of 1707. I. The Economic Background. *The Economic History Review* 16 (3): 455–467.

Somers, J. 1730. *The True Secret History of the Lives of All the Kings and Queens of England*, 2 vols. London: D. Browne.

Watt, D. 2014. *The Price of Scotland: Darien, Union, and the Wealth of Nations*. Edinburgh: Luath Press Ltd.

Whately, C. 2008. *The Scots and the Union*. New York: Columbia University Press.

3

Beyond Trade: Mercantilist Ideas of Dependency, Value, and Transmutation and Justification of Union

Abstract This chapter explores how the writings of the three most influential mercantilist writers, Thomas Mun, Charles Davenant, and William Petty, supported the idea that Scotland was a "dependent" country that should join with England. Mun's discussion of trade as the origin of value and authority demonstrates the notion that wealth is tied to one's total volume of trade. Davenant's work is pivotal in arguing for what makes a nation dependent and independent. His arguments regarding trade and national defense are applied to Scotland. Petty's work is explored for its use of political arithmetic to justify particular policy positions and for the concept of transmutation, or how to create a union not by joining two nations together but by transforming the less productive into the more productive.

Keywords Thomas Mun • Charles Davenant • William Petty • Trade • Value • Dependency • Transmutation • Authority • Money • Mercantilism • Scotland • National defense • Transplantation • Political arithmetic

A. Ramos, *Shifting Capital*, Palgrave Studies in the History of Economic Thought,
https://doi.org/10.1007/978-3-319-96403-4_3

Issues of sovereignty, trade, and defense pervaded both the discussions of the Parliament of 1703 and the eventual move toward union. Why did the English and Scottish commissioners who supported union believe that Scotland neither should maintain full sovereignty nor could alleviate its economic issues without an incorporating union? A commercial union was a feasible solution to create a strong external trade sector, and yet was not considered to be so by the majority of the ministers of both parliaments. Pervasive ideas of the period regarding what made a nation viable and independent are very relevant to understanding the movement to union by members of both parliaments. Apart from the political and security concerns of the English, an explanation is found regarding views of national strength and independence in the representative mercantilist in the works of Thomas Mun and Charles Davenant. From an English mercantilist perspective, there was more than just a weak trade sector at play in their assessment of Scotland's potential as an independent entity. From an economic viewpoint, the prevailing mercantilist view of what conferred authority and sovereignty is essential. The theory of trade and theory of sovereignty, or its opposite of dependency, explain the reason why Scotland was perceived to be unable to survive even in a federal union. The notion of an incorporating union itself as the solution to the problems on both sides also has its roots in mercantilism, as a recurrent idea in the work of William Petty is transmutation, of which the Union is an application.

With the adoption of these views on trade, value, and dependency, mercantilism is being wielded in a new way, but for the same purposes as it always had: to ensure that England emerged from any conflict with an advantage. Whether the negotiators truly believed the view of Scotland that emerges from the application of the mercantilist principles here, or simply used these ideas as justification for their actions to achieve their political goals, the construction of an argument that a nation is dependent and must have its sovereignty limited rather than expanded, by being transformed into another political entity altogether, can be seen as structural violence.

3.1 Trade, Value, and Authority

Although centered on trade, the mercantilist worldview used trade and commercial power simply as a means to an end. While it is true that some writers did conflate the circulation of money with the circulation of a capital stock and thus mistake the true engine of the economic growth of the nation, all mercantilist authors were focused on growth as an expression of national power and a point of comparison with other nations. The main rival of English commercial power and thus of nation-building in the seventeenth century was the Netherlands. Early mercantilist writing sought to uncover both what had made the Dutch so economically successful and how to use those tools not only to England's best advantage but also to overtake the other country in supremacy of the seas.

In *England's Treasure by Foreign Trade*, Mun discusses trade itself, or, more specifically, loss of advantage in trade in violent terms in his discussion of the Dutch ascendancy over the English in any market:

> But if any man allege the Dutch proverb, Live and let others live; I answer, that the Dutchmen notwithstanding their own Proverb, doe not only in these Kingdoms, encroach upon our livings, but also in other forraign parts of our trade (where they have power) they do hinder and destroy us in our lawful course of living, hereby taking the bread out of our mouth, which we shall never prevent by plucking the pot from their nose … We ought rather to imitate former times in taking sober and worthy course more pleasing to God and suitable to our ancient reputation. (p. 35)

What Mun recommends is not a cessation of trade altogether with the Dutch, "plucking the pot from under their nose," but rather in this same section argues that punitive taxes on English products made with foreign inputs be repealed. Rather than punishing domestic producers for using less expensive inputs from overseas, it was fitting, according to Mun, to let the English manufacturers use the inputs to produce more goods and export them back to trade rivals. This would both increase England's employment and prosperity and cause a loss to foreign competitors buying the finished products.

The mercantilist rationale here is the familiar one that a country is wealthy if its exports exceed its imports, which also employs the concept of the balance, or again a surplus rather than an even balance. As director of the East India Company, Mun had personal reasons of course for espousing his theory. He stressed that trade was the source of the power of the nation. However, rather than an export surplus, Mun stressed that all trade was beneficial to a nation if imports were used to create later manufactured goods and exports. He thus took a longer-term view on the wealth that a trade imbalance might create. Additionally, he held to the martial aspect of mercantilism that it was necessary to have a larger volume of trade than one's rivals.

It is also salient that Mun wrote *England's Treasure* in the midst of an English coinage crisis and recession. James VI called a committee to investigate the crisis composed of the master of the Royal Mint, Gerard Malynes, the director of the Merchant Adventurers' Company, Edward Misselden, and Mun. Mary Poovey (1998) explains that the discussions of the three as to how the monetary shortage could be resolved and whether the value of the coin should be changed are about trade but also about the generation of value. Is the authority that confers value the government or the king himself, as argued by Malynes in his call to have the coin revalued at a rate set by the king and overseen by the mint? Or does it arise from trade, as argued by Misselden and Mun, from processes known somewhat to merchants but mostly to forces that are not fully knowable? Mun's and Malynes' conclusions made a major contribution to the development of economic thought on trade as they argued that the favorable balance of trade, and thus the balance of payments, the country had previously enjoyed had shifted. Trade, they argued, should be the focus of analysis rather than the authority of the king to recoin the money and alter exchange rates. By focusing on the balance of trade rather than simply the ability of the king to change the monetary situation through recoinage, Mun offered a mechanical interpretation of the foundation of the nation's power. The power of commercial activity rather than the power of the monarch to interfere with the value of money or the money supply is what confers value (pp. 68–91).

The discussion of the source of value is relevant here not only in terms of theory but also because the competition between England and Scotland can be seen not only as a contest for an export surplus and resources to use as inputs, but also over the creation of value. An additional reason therefore emerges as to why the English sought to limit Scotland's trade. The logic is the same as when examining a quantity of goods generated by a trade surplus, but here it is in terms of the market value of goods exchanging hands. There is an assumption that the field of trade and the total possibilities of trade are limited and must be taken or ensure that others cannot do so. By not allowing Scotland's merchants access to the source of increased value creation, England could always maintain its position as the wealthier of the two countries.

A subtler argument for the necessity of Union can also be seen. If value is generated by government authority or by peoples' faith in the stability of a government, Scotland has a government in its own parliament that can perform that function. But if value is generated through external trade, an argument can be made that the country will never attain economic growth because its trade is limited and what trade it has is stagnating. This is not to argue that Mun is wrong in his assertion about the source of value, but only to observe that this theory of value generates a reason why many ministers on both sides assumed that Scotland's economy was incapable of generating long-term growth outside of the Union. Trade by definition is a necessity if the calculation of the wealth of the nation depends upon it.

As Pocock (1975) previously observed in the work of the mercantilists, but Davenant in particular, trade is what gives land value, and is just as necessary as civic virtue to sustain the commonwealth (p. 442). Petty has a similar concept in his political arithmetic in trying to develop a par between land and labor, such that the value of land could be expressed in terms of the output of labor, albeit unsuccessful as Mirowski pointed out in finding what substance exactly makes these two equal (p. 154). In the framework of Davenant and Petty, land has no value apart from trade. Therefore, a country without trade is a country with diminished wealth in land. Without extensive access to external trade, the landed estates of Scotland cannot generate rejuvenation for the country on their own and the Union is a way out, a way to give "real" value to Scottish property by denominating it in pounds sterling and exporting more of its output. And to consider not by whom it was owned but by how much it or its yield was worth in the market.

While Mun's basic argument does not seem either injurious to Scottish independence or connected to the arguments for Union, the time in which Mun's most famous pamphlet was published and circulated is relevant to both of these. *England's Treasure by Forraign Trade* was published posthumously by Mun's son. At the time, England was in a trade war with the Dutch and the pamphlet was used in the mobilization of opinion in favor of English trade policies that would build the nation's exports, support the trading companies, and create a position of superiority to the Dutch (Magnusson 1994, pp. 59–60).

How this outlook relates to the Scottish situation at the wake of the Union negotiations is that from the English perspective, stabilization and growth of Scottish trade was perceived as a threat. From the Scottish perspective, to proponents of the Union the mercantilist focus on trade as the major means of growth simply illuminated Scotland's poverty within this paradigm, and for those opposed to the Union it also shone a light on the ways in which current trade policy strangled Scotland's external trade and a Union would alter the pattern of Scotland's traditional trade alliances, which was one of its key sources of economic growth.

3.2 Trade, Defense, and Dependency

Besides the United Provinces another nation that looms large in the writing of the late seventeenth-century pamphleteers, especially in the case of Petty and Charles Davenant, is Ireland. The Irish question arises due to the reassertion of Irish writers of the political independence of their country, as they have never been fully conquered and were never officially made a colony, as William Molyneux (1698) asserted in *Case of Ireland Stat'd*. In answer to these facts, a thread of reasoning emerges in mercantilist writing regarding what truly makes a country independent. These arguments revolve around economic self-sufficiency that allows for an accumulation of resources such that a country is also able to defend itself against its enemies, and the ability to make laws. While William Petty identifies Ireland as poor and provides an analysis of why and how its resources can be reallocated, Davenant provides the justification for why Ireland cannot be freed from English administrative control.

Both Davenant and Petty promote English control as a solution for Ireland's poverty. The argument for Irish dependency is directly relevant to the Scottish situation on the eve of the Union, not because Scotland experienced the level of poverty that Ireland did, but because the line of reasoning that is used in the one case is used more subtly but asserted all the same in the other: because it currently lacks the ability to provide the revenue to provide for its own defense, external trade, and domestic self-sufficiency, Scotland should not remain an independent nation. The solution offered is also the same, although again slightly altered in its form: administrative change and transmutation of Scottish norms and economic institutions.

Charles Davenant contributed to mercantilist theory but his motives were not necessarily for the purity of theory. As he sought to regain a position in the English administration, his work often justifies extant English policy. Sometimes this was at the behest of English ministers. For instance, John Somers relates that *Peace at Home, and War Abroad* was written on request, "tho not commonly known, by the Lord-Treasurer Godolphin," who was later a commissioner for Union (1730, p. 283). Either independently or as a government agent, Davenant is the architect and defender of the trade theories that maintained English dominance of trade among the Three Kingdoms. Besides the standard argument to maintain a positive trade balance, Davenant introduces a new defense for the dominance of one country over others. He makes arguments regarding dependency and independence that are repeated in the pamphlet literature of the period and reflected in the policy positions England adopts vis-à-vis Ireland and Scotland. Davenant's arguments are outlined in several pamphlets from the 1690s: *An Essay on Ways and Means of Supplying the War* (1695), the *Essay on the East India Trade* (1697) *Discourses on the Public Revenue* (1698), and *Making People Gainers in the Balance of Trade* (1699). He writes in answer to Molyneux's assertion that Ireland cannot be a political dependency of England because it was not a conquered country and should be given the right to rule itself without requiring its decisions to be approved by the English parliament. Molyneux's argument had great implications for trade. With increased political sovereignty Ireland would be able to circumvent the Navigation Acts that severely curtailed Ireland's ability to engage in overseas trade.

Davenant moves the grounds of the argument from the political to the economic by establishing his criteria for independence, which is ability to provide economically for oneself, having overseas trade, and the ability for self-defense. Ireland depends on England for its economic maintenance and for its defense and therefore cannot be treated as a sovereign nation. Restrictions on Ireland's trade, Davenant argues in the *Discourses on the Public Revenues*, will "hurt but a very few [in Ireland], (which is never to be regarded, where the good of the whole public is in question)" (p. 254). His prediction for Ireland is that even "though a large part of our trade be diverted thither, they would not yet be able to subsist alone and by themselves" (1699, p. 250). The ability of Ireland to "subsist alone and by themselves" depends not only on keeping their costs of production low, but also on being able to pay for their own defense: "And since War is grown so expensive, and Trade is become so extended; and since Luxury has so much obtain'd in the World, no Nation can subsist of it self without Helps and Aids from other places" (1695, p. 13). Ireland should remain a colony for its own benefit, "because it gives them a lasting title to be defended and protected by us" (1699, p. 250). Thus, he concludes it is in the best interests of both countries that England craft trade regulations and provide military defense for hapless, dependent Ireland (p. 251). Even if Ireland is able to defend itself as a commercial republic against other commercial republics, it would still not be able to defend itself in the arena of modern warfare. Ironically, he defends the restrictions of the Navigation Acts by referring to the threat of Ireland's capacity to have a stronger economy. If the free export of wool were allowed from Ireland, however, "their wealth would be built on our destruction" (p. 255).

Davenant also has a very particular view of wealth. In his method of national income accounting, he concludes that the national wealth is that which is the total output produced minus everything consumed domestically and minus the amount spent by the government on public goods. Finkelstein notes that wealth according to this logic is "investment plus net exports" (p. 230). Another way to view Davenant's conception of wealth is that it is equal to all the goods available to export and all that that is available for use to make more exports. Therefore, a country like Ireland with a low external trade cannot be wealthy, and Scotland after the loss of Darien is in a similar low-wealth situation. Additionally, any increase in government expenditure on national defense, as would be necessary in Ireland's case, would simply deplete the national wealth. Given Davenant's limiting worldview, it is also not possible for Ireland, which he observes also suffers from unemployment, to make up the lack of production by manufacturing export oriented goods because its population is too low to make up for the lack in the production of finished goods for export. A fully independent country is one that has the resources to produce and export goods, maintain a trade surplus, defend its trading activity and domestic territory, and have a variety of excises to draw from in order to do so. As he was also eager for a reappointment in William and Anne's administrations, Davenant's justification of English policy toward Ireland, and indeed any other country from which it needed to draw raw materials or export its surplus, is colored by a need to uphold the current military and political power structure.

"Can a Nation be safe without strength?" Davenant asks in the *Essay on the East India Trade*:

> And is power to be compassed and secured but by riches? And can a country become rich any way, but by the help of a well managed and extended traffick?... we could not have grown rich without other dealings with the world. (p. 7)

He then argues that England has been able to sustain its position in the war for so long only due to the inflow of wealth from trade. To Davenant it is not enough in the late seventeenth century for a country to simply have commercial capital; it must also have military capability. However, the latter is tied to the former. A state that has the revenue from trade and the ability to raise taxes on incomes that are rising due to trade has more financial capital at its disposal to finance a navy and a standing army. Because these both require more funds than a state may have on hand to pay for those particular expenditures, the state also needs to have the ability to borrow large amounts, which requires credit which is dependent on confidence in one's ability to pay back large amounts. Therefore, England chartered the Bank of England so as not to be beholden to individual private lenders or nobles but to an institution created for the purpose of financing mercantilist projects, whether they be a standing army or the development of shipping for the carrying trade. Davenant, as Pocock notes, makes an argument typical of the era: Naval warfare is more cost-effective than battles on land, and will thus be less injurious to the national debt, and has the added benefit of hurting Spanish and French trade (p. 442). Again, the concepts of war, commerce, and cost are intertwined.

3.3 Poverty and Population

Scotland's alleged poverty was also an argument used for joining a union. Some accounts have argued that the country's economic picture was not as dire as previously reported (MacInnes 2007; Devine 2003, 2016). However, the mercantilist view of poverty differs from that of simply producing a certain amount of output or of having a stable food supply; and, thus, when arguments were made regarding poverty, they did not necessarily refer to internal stability or sustainability. The mercantilist view of poverty rests upon the availability of people and natural resources. "Fewness of people," Petty writes in *A Treatise of Taxes and Contributions* (1662), "is real poverty," and "if the people be so few that they can live Ex sponte Creatis, or with little labour, such as grazing, etc. they become wholly without Art" (p. 34). When natural resources are abundant and the country is reasonably populated however, as in the cases of Ireland and Scotland, and the country continues to be poor, the next level of explanation is that the population is too lazy to put their resources to use. One can see this in the literature regarding Ireland's economic conditions. Rather than structural violence imposed through English trade policy, absentee landlords, and lack of local administrative control over the country, the cause of Ireland's poverty was continually, and conveniently, laid at its own feet by English pamphleteers.

A similar thread runs through the propaganda concerning Scotland and the Union. A representative example of this line of reasoning in relation to Scotland can be found in Defoe's poem *Caledonia*, which he wrote as part of a propaganda offensive to convince the Scottish ministers to approve the treaty. Ostensibly a paean to Scotland and its people, the poem contains an argument for why the Union is the best means of generating economic improvement for the country. Lack of opportunities had caused the country to lose population to the colonies and enlistment in armies overseas. Development of the fisher and other industries, as promised by the Union, would draw people back to their homeland, Defoe reasons. He identifies sloth as the cause of Scotland's woes, "but not your major crime" (p. 57) because sloth and poverty reinforced each other, as "poverty makes sloth and sloth makes poor" (p. 58). The low level of economic development creates "sloth" because there is no incentive to industry, further exacerbating a lack of production. "Success alone can quicken industry," he says, and an outside force will have to accomplish this to create incentives to productivity (p. 59). There is no reason for Scotland to be poor as he sees "No barrenness but in your industry" (p. 57). He recommends that the landed gentry improve their lands, develop the fishing and shipping industries, and vote for the Union. A development of infrastructure to support the "treasure of the fishery" (p. 12) would allow the use of this "unexhausted" resource, large enough "to subsist the whole country" (p. 16, note F). Rather than conquering territory by developing a navy and colonies, he encourages the country to look inward to conquer its poverty and develop the fishery and the other industries that the English promised to invest in if the Union were approved. The suggested development policy in order to retain population is not a bad one, but it is also one that does not necessarily require full political union for its accomplishment.

Population growth was also beneficial because it resulted in the expansion of urban centers. Petty made this argument by comparing England's larger urban population to Ireland's, the majority of whom were concentrated in London and Dublin, respectively. Both cities, he argues, were stronger economically than other parts of the countries but the higher number of people in London caused it to be more economically robust than Dublin. The concentration of population in urban areas, he argued, caused a higher demand for luxuries and their production and would make production more efficient, "the inhabitants of cities and towns, spend more [on] commodities, and make greater consumptions, than those who live in wild thin peopled countries" (quoted in Fox 2009, pp. 399–400).

3.4 The Stock of Resources

Davenant likens the resources of the country, both physical and natural, what he refers to as the "stock," to the moisture in a body. In fact, he calls it "the radical moisture of the commonwealth." When drawn away and not replenished, the body suffers. Trade, Davenant offers, is a remedy to this dehydration, "so nations cannot subsist long unless they receive from time to time reliefs and refreshments from abroad, which are no way so well to be administered as by the help of a well governed and extended Traffic" (1698, p. 75).

He argues that England has increased its wealth and stock through the East India Trade since 1688, both from goods exported thence and also from inputs imported and used for manufactured goods for export, and that "whatever country can be in the full and undisputed possession of it, will give law to all the commercial world." If the Dutch should take it over, he cautions that "England must hereafter be contented to trade by their protection and under their banners" (1697, p. 94). Rather than trade being at the service of government, all is turned to trade: "The wisdom of the legislative power consists ... to promote all, and chiefly to encourage such trades, as increase the public stock, and add to the kingdoms wealth, considered as a collective body" (p. 98). The pursuit of the kingdom's wealth and power is the goal.

However, Petty says that it is not enough to consider a country's population and resources "when the Question is concerning their Wealth and Strength; It is also material to examine, how many of them do get more than they spend and how many less" (p. 291). The reasons why are twofold. One has to do with basic subsistence, whether a people could provide for themselves, and the other with whether they have enough left over to produce goods for trade and for defense. Petty provides further justifications for union and a solution to the problem of the lack of resources and trade, but in discussing having a fund beyond subsistence also alludes to financial resources.

Although they do not always treat it as such, finance was another resource, or a means to make natural resources liquid. Mobility of property in the form of money and credit was on the rise also in the seventeenth century, providing the mental space to conceive of movements of other kinds of capital. Pocock comments that for Davenant the value of everything in an economy that requires public finance is dependent on how quickly financial capital can be acquired (p. 451). With the expansion of financial institutions in Scotland, the country had both its own sources of credit and competition for English financial investment. Union was a means to increase the credit and financial resources available to England.

Connecting the discussion of population and other resources back to value illuminates the arguments for the union. It is trade that gives land its value according to Davenant. Petty earlier tried to use labor as the common denominator of value. Each pursues a constant in the system according to standard mercantilist thought. If population is the wealth of the nation, then the laboring population must be the true denominator of value, as is Petty's argument. If the volume of trade is the wealth of the nation, then trade must be the underlying value substance in the economy, as is argued by Davenant. In either case it could be argued that Scotland was losing its value through its loss of population to emigration to the plantations and enlistment in overseas armies, or that due to its decreasing volume of trade, regardless of the source of that decline being English legislation. A more extensive trade would arguably allow Scotland access to more resources. Thus, to restore trade and population both was to increase the wealth of the nation and the Union promised to do both.

3.5 Reallocation and Transmutation

Another means of increasing the wealth of the nation in Petty's work was through a movement of resources and a transformation of interests. He argues that based on efficiency one of England's "impediments of greatness" is that there are too many legislative governments: England, Scotland, Ireland, and the colonies and plantations. Besides a diffusion of government and differing governance structures, "small divided remote governments are seldom able to defend themselves, the burthen of protecting of them all, must lye upon the chief Kingdom England; and so all the smaller kingdoms and dominions, instead of being Additions are really Diminutions" (1755, p. 163). His solution is to create a united government composed of two councils, one of which is chosen by the king and the other by the people.

The reason for a united government from Petty's political arithmetic point of view is because the differing governments are "an impediment to wealth" (p. 163). He identifies the wealth of the nation as the wealth of its subjects, the part of the subjects' wealth given for "the public defense, honour, and ornament of the people," and the portion of the wealth given to the government that is the king's to dispose of as he sees fit. Petty specifies the "distances and differences" of the kingdoms and dominions as the major problem. In a time of war, England would bear the major, if not total, burden of national defense of all the others. Because of having different regional governments, England's restrictions on imports from the others caused the prices of finished goods using imports to increase or caused an increase in imports of finished goods from Holland and France who were able to purchase cheaper Irish and Scottish goods for inputs. Customs duties were unnecessarily complicated among all the countries of the British Isles. Colonial merchant costs were increased because all goods had to pass through English ports and on English ships before being sold in the colonies and plantations (pp. 164–169). Petty favored full political union with Ireland in order to eliminate warfare and its costs and a united government to lower costs and increase the total productivity of both. This idea is easily applied to Scotland.

3.5.1 Political Anatomy, Transmutation, and Transplantation

A clear pattern regarding how to increase a country's productivity emerges in Petty's works from the *Political Anatomy* to the *Essays in Political Arithmetic*. Petty produced the *Down Survey*, which became the *Political Anatomy of Ireland*, as a result of being tasked in 1653 to assess the values of the forfeited lands of Irish rebels so they could be distributed to the English troops loyal to Cromwell, who had put down the Irish rebellion. Petty surveyed Ireland on the basis of value and redistribution of resources.

By basing his division of the lands on economic rather than political and religious categories, the political difficulties of how to deal with rebellion and reward were solved. Petty reapplies this concept in his later suggestions regarding low economic growth in Ireland and Highland Scotland and further potential rebellion from the native Irish (1691, pp. 228–229). Each can be solved through an assessment of what is contributing to the problem and a redistribution of these elements in some manner that will benefit England. In *Political Anatomy*, Petty's solution to economic issues and rebellion is "the transmuting one People into the other, and the thorough union of interests upon natural and lasting Principles" (1691, p. 157). Thus, the idea of conquering another nation without military expenditure reappears not in trade but in transformation. These concepts can also be seen in the concept of the Union.

Ted McCormick (2006, 2009) shows that Petty's concerns were not only mechanical or related to resources but that he also saw political anatomy as a means of identifying and resolving potential political issues. Through an analysis and categorization of Ireland's population, Petty had identified Ireland's economic issues as being one of an excess of Irishness (2006, p. 294). His solution was to transmute the Irish into English. He proposed to do this by transplanting a certain number of Englishwomen into Irish households. The resulting relationships would produce children who would be raised with English sensibilities because mothers, Petty assumed, played the major role in the education of children. A transmission of values would then occur over successive generations and the Irishness bred out of them. Thus, the next generation would have imbued in them English interests.

In *Essays in Political Arithmetic*, Petty also focuses not on a transformation of households but on the transplantation of many peoples. He promotes a transfer of people from the poorest parts of Ireland and the entire population of the Scottish Highlands to less populated regions of England, Wales, and Lowland Scotland and to move the completely undesirable and unproductive to the colonies. This scheme of transference is possible, he claims, if the Lowlands, England, and Wales can produce more food, estimated by him to be for one-fifth of a greater population than presently. If so, then the people of Ireland and the Highlands will not be a burden on these lands and will be better off. The assumption is of course that the lands of Ireland and the Highlands cannot be as productive as the other three locations. He reasons if the value of the immovable resources left behind in Ireland and the Highlands are less than the value of "the advancement of the price of land in England," then it is a reasonable proposal. Additionally, if the immovable and the "relict" land left behind can be sold for money and that the nation who purchases them will not cause more "Transplantees" to be moved into England than previously, then again the scheme is beneficial (pp. 228–229).

He calculated the total cost of transplantation as £17 million by adding the loss of the houses and land in Ireland and Scotland to the cost of transporting persons to England, the Lowlands, and Wales. The benefit, "about Sixty Nine millions, three hundred thousand pounds," far exceeds the cost (p. 231). He arrives at this number by calculating the increase in land rents due to the expected increase in population and multiplying by a lease of 17 years. The total increase of persons will be 180,000 people "from the poor and miserable Trade of Husbandry to more beneficial Handicrafts." The marginal addition of persons to the same arable land will produce more than one-fifth of what it currently produces and therefore will be enough to feed the newcomers and the current population (pp. 232–233). With the transfer of people into manufactures and away from husbandry, their incomes will increase, causing more expenditure. Although he previously states that the Transplantees will be moved to England, the Lowlands, and Wales, in the final analysis Petty's biases are clear: "So when England shall be thicker peopled in the manner before described, the same people" will spend and produce more and also "desire to put on better Apparel when he appears in Company, than when he has no occasion to be seen" (p. 233). The last would be a boon to the English textile industry. He also concludes that the cost of public administration would fall, as the civil and military government would no longer have to make expenditures in these far-flung and troublesome locations (p. 248).

The Union is an application of Petty's idea of both transmutation and transplantation. In terms of transplantation, the Union represents a movement of resources from one place to another, of capital resources both into and out of Scotland. The transmutation of Scotland did not have to be as complete as Petty had suggested for Ireland. Defoe pointed out in *Caledonia* that the Scots had never rebelled against the monarch as the Irish had. Certain social institutions were left intact. The legal system in Scotland was left to operate as it had, excepting of course on matters that related to Britain as a whole, and the Scottish Kirk was allowed to maintain its independence. What were required to change, however, were the elements of command, control, and resource use: the location of the capital, the location and structure of parliament, and thus power over revenue and policy. The method of the Union is the same as Petty's transplantation of Irish and Highlanders into England: redistribution of assets such that one attains the situation one desires. The purpose of the Union is the same as Petty's purpose of moving Englishwomen into Irish homes: to create a joint interest. If the Scottish become British, then their interests will be allied fully with the English. Because the English would have the advantage in terms of physical and political resources, the interests that would dominate would also be England's. Thus, the Scottish interest would become English interest. Rather than a movement of persons, the Union involved a movement of borders, economic institutions, and political institutions or political capital.

How these assets were to be moved and how the arrangement benefitted England, although on paper they seemed to advantage Scotland, as well as the recurrence of the themes of trade, defense, and dependency, are examined in the treaty negotiations and the Articles of Union in the next chapter.

References

Davenant, C. [1697] 1771. Essay on the East India Trade. In *Political and Commercial Works*, ed. C. Whitworth, vol. 1, 83–126. London: T. Cadell.

———. [1698] 1771. Discourses on the Public Revenues and Trade of England. In *Political and Commercial Works*, ed. C. Whitworth, vol. 2, 1–76. London: T. Cadell.

———. [1699] 1771. An Essay on Ways and Means of Supplying the War. In *Political and Commercial Works*, ed. C. Whitworth, vol. 1, 1–82. London: T. Cadell.

Defoe, D. 1706. *Caledonia: A Poem in Honour of the Scots and the Scots Nation.* Edinburgh: Andrew Anderson.

Devine, T.M. 2003. *Scotland's Empire, 1600–1815*. London: Allen Lane.
———. 2016. *Independence or Union: Scotland's Past and Scotland's Present*. London: Penguin.
Finkelstein, A. 2000. *Harmony and the Balance: An Intellectual History of the Seventeenth Century*. Ann Arbor: University of Michigan Press.
Fox, A. 2009. Sir William Petty, Ireland, and the Making of a Political Economist. *Economic History Review* 62 (2): 388–404.
MacInnes, A. 2007. *Union and Empire: The Making of the United Kingdom in 1707*. Cambridge: Cambridge University Press.
Magnusson, L. 1994. *Mercantilism: The Shaping of an Economic Language*. London: Routledge.
McCormick, T. 2006. Alchemy in the Political Arithmetic of William Petty. *Studies in the History and Philosophy of Science* 37 (2): 290–307.
———. 2009. *William Petty and the Ambitions of Political Arithmetic*. Oxford: Oxford University Press.
Mirowski, P. 1989. *More Heat Than Light*. Cambridge: Cambridge University Press.
Molyneux, W. 1698. *The Case of Ireland's Being Bound by Acts of Parliament in England, Stated*. Dublin: Joseph Ray.
Mun, T. 1664. *England's Treasure by Forraign Trade*. London: Thomas Clark.
Petty, W. [1691] 1899. The Political Anatomy of Ireland. In *Economic Writings of William Petty*, ed. C. Hull, 121–231. London: Cambridge University Press.
———. 1755. *Several Essays in Political Arithmetick*. 4th ed. London: D. Browne.
_______. [1662] 1899. A Treatise on Taxes and Contributions. In *Economic Writings of William Petty*, ed. C. Hull, 1–97. London: Cambridge University Press.
Pocock, J.G.A. 1975. *The Machiavellian Moment*. Princeton: Princeton University Press.
Poovey, M. 1998. *A History of the Modern Fact*. Chicago: University of Chicago Press.
Somers, J. 1730. *The True Secret History of the Lives of All the Kings and Queens of England*, 2 vols. London: D. Browne.

4

Trick or Treaty: The Negotiation and Articles of Union in the Context of Mercantilist Ideas

Abstract This chapter examines the economics of the Articles of Union, integrating the concepts of positive balance to assess what each side hoped to gain, and structural violence to analyze how England prevented Scotland from getting any advantage over itself. The articles on economic issues such as taxation, debt, and the Equivalent are explored both at the drafting stage and in the debates in the Scottish Parliament before their passage. The articles on the dissolution of the parliament, the Company of Scotland, and movement of the capital are also discussed for their long-term economic implications. In particular, the issue of reduced representation for Scotland is analyzed as a form of structural violence wherein Scotland was ensured of never attaining a majority over their English counterparts.

Keywords Act of Union • Parliament • Structural violence • Representation • Taxation • Articles of Union • Debt • Equivalent • John Somers • John Clerk • George Lockhart • Earl of Stair • Union treaty • Political capital

A. Ramos, *Shifting Capital*, Palgrave Studies in the History of Economic Thought,
https://doi.org/10.1007/978-3-319-96403-4_4

In this chapter I wish to examine in mercantilist terms what it was that each side fought for in the initial negotiations and the parliamentary debate upon the Articles of Union. While it is clear, as from past literature, that the Scottish commissioners argued for free trade with England and the colonies, what has been less examined is how the English commissioners' ensured England gained advantage from the treaty. Security on their northern border is certainly one benefit the Union offered, but from the negotiations and the memoir of John Somers, the main architect of the articles, it can be seen that the articles were purposefully crafted to give England an advantage over its neighbor in economics and politics. The very act of requiring a full incorporating union and dismissal of other options was an act of structural violence. As is argued in a pamphlet by English commissioner Somers, the addition of Scotland to England was seen not so much as the creation of a new country but as the elimination of a political problem and the absorption of capital and people: "so much will there be added to the stock of England" (1705, p. 9). Defoe says similarly in his pamphlet on the union, "In this Union here are lands and people added to the *English* empire" (1706, p. 5; emphasis Defoe's). Mercantilist thinking pervaded theories, analyses, and the construction of the Articles of Union. In order to agree to the Union, both sides felt they had to be gaining some surplus of advantage compared to their neighbor. How this idea manifested is examined in Somers' essay about the Union, in particular articles, and in the final Scottish parliamentary debates.

4.1 John Somers and the Mercantilist Reasoning of the Articles

The structural violence of mercantilism was at play previous to the drafting of the articles as seen in Lord Sidney Godolphin's creation of the Alien Act. Previously, William's High Chancellor and member of the Board of Treasury Godolphin was appointed as Anne's chief commissioner for Union. Familiar with both statecraft and public finance, he had already shown by the Alien Act that he could force a negotiation to turn out to England's advantage.

While Godolphin was instrumental in the mercantilist means of edging the Scottish ministers to the negotiation table, it was the Lord High Chancellor John Somers who played a pivotal role in the negotiations and drafting of the articles. Bishop Gilbert Burnet (1840), another English commissioner, confirms that Somers "had the chief hand in projecting the scheme of the union" and that the other English commissioners easily followed his lead (p. 799). Somers' original intentions regarding the Union are presented in a pamphlet that was printed in both England and Scotland anonymously and under a different title, in 1705. He proposes that the Scots be allowed to keep their Kirk and its governance, as should the Church of England, as "the Union both nations have occasion for, is to be made up of none of these forms and matters, but must arise out of a Communication of Trade, and a unity of peace and war in both kingdoms." He then argues that the Union ought to contain a united parliament, "unity in trade and taxes," and "unity in the public administration of the revenues of both kingdoms" (p. 2). All of these were included in the final articles that were passed. While the political expediency of these elements have been analyzed before, the economic efficiency of such from the mercantilist perspective has not.

Somers' main argument for union rests not on politics but on economics and public finance. His main concerns are trade and war, and the ability to gain an advantage in one and to finance the other, which then confers its own advantages. The regal union conferred the right to conduct peace and war for both kingdoms, Somers says, and that he need not argue this point further. However:

> the right of giving money for the support of the war is uncontestably lodged with the people assembled in Parliament ... and since both Nations are involved in one and the same fate of war and peace, it's but reasonable that the people of both nations should be heard in one and the same Parliament ... or at least before they part with their Money or Men for the support of one or the keeping of the other. (p. 2)

He calls for Scots to be called in both the House and the Lords but for the ministers of England to not have a vote on matters that pertain only to Scotland and vice versa for the Scottish ministers. Although he proposes a confederal governance whereby there would still be a Scottish Parliament in addition to the united parliament, Somers' claims that the English will benefit from going to serve in the Scots' parliament due to increased opportunity for "alliances, friendships and marriages, and for the improvement of trade, and encouragement of arts and sciences" (p. 3). However, the Scots, he argues, would suffer from doing the opposite because it would carry money out of the country. This is also why he believes the proposed 56 Scottish ministers for the new parliament is a reasonable number. To have the same amount of representation as the Scottish people currently enjoyed would hurt them financially and also allow their nobility to continue to have a disproportionate amount of influence over Scottish affairs. Although the English ministers will outnumber them, the Scots have nothing to fear as all would be of one nation, "and have but one and the same interest" (p. 3). The similarities to Petty's arguments discussed in Chap. 3 regarding transmutation and the conversion of interests are clear.

The last part of Somers' proposal is to create a Court of Revenue in Scotland to prosecute abuses to the national revenue (p. 7). This was a necessity, he argues, simply because the English institutions are better: "The constitution and method of the Treasury, the Exchequer, the customs and excises of England are so far superior to anything of these kinds that are to be found in Scotland" (p. 9). He expected the Scots to happily let go of their own institutions and be grateful that their countrymen would be able to attain these new positions of government.

Scottish land and trade will both benefit from the Union, he says, and provide the variables by which this can be quantified: "value and rent" for land, and "extent and bulk" for trade (9). He then makes an extremely mercantilist remark that "so much as there is of land in Scotland and how much that land is improvable, or how much the trade of Scotland is increasable, so much will there be added to the stock of England" (9). It is understandable that he would explain the benefit to England in a pamphlet published to increase English support, but the fact remains that the focus is on both trade and the power accruing to the nation. The economic improvement of Scotland in this paragraph is tied, not to the improvement of quality of life for the Scottish people, but to an increase in their ability to pay taxes for future wars, as he reasons, the Scots' ability to pay higher land taxes and customs excises will increase as the value of their lands increase.

Above all, he says readers are to consider, "That upon the day they are united with England, the value of the land in Scotland will rise fifty per cent and in progress of time will double, nay treble the present rental" (p. 9). Just as earlier when he asserts value and rent will rise simply due to the Union, he does not explain why. These increases in rent however will increase the price of food, but due to the increase in trade with England, more money would be available to pay for it and other goods, "ten times faster than at the low rate" (p. 9). This assertion is based on nothing more than what had happened during the years of Cromwell's rule when there was a supposed unity of government, at least insofar as the pamphlet says. An actual reason why land rent would increase is because the demand for Scottish goods would cause the value of those goods to increase and thus for the produce of the land to increase.

He also reassured his readers that although the Scots would not have to pay additional duties and customs within Scotland for goods imported to that country, they would have to pay additional taxes if importing goods into any port in England, even if they had already paid the basic customs duty for importation of the good into Scotland. Somers concludes, "Thus the balance of trade will after the Union remain as before the Union, and what the Scots save on their customs and excises is always to be understood of their home consumption within the present district of Scotland" (p. 9).

The costs to England for the Union would be a minimal increase in payments for the salaries of the customs and excise administrators, civil administrators, and the guards and garrisons, estimated to be a mere £13,360 per year (p. 9).

Somers claims in his conclusion to have been impartial to both countries in his essay, a claim made, as seen in Chap. 3, of political arithmetic. Use of the language of trade and benefits focuses on quantifiables rather than persons or political gains and losses. While it may confer the semblance of impartiality, Somers' use of mercantilist political arithmetic rhetoric illuminates his goals, which is the maximization of wealth and power of the English state, to be accomplished by increased resources, trade, customs duties, and tax collection that would increase the state revenue and thus the ability to conduct war and protect commercial interests. The proposal for the continuance of the Scottish Parliament also seems to confer impartiality, but it was not included in the negotiations or in the final treaty.

Interestingly, Somers' proposals for united and separate parliaments align with Petty's proposed plan of union for England and Ireland. The rationale for having members sit in each other's parliaments is to eliminate partiality. In the *Political Anatomy*, Petty says, "if both kingdoms were under one legislative power and parliament, the members whereof should be propotionable in power and wealth of each nation" (1769, p. 322). Neither side could show partiality to their own country if both have representatives in each other's parliaments.

As a minister of state, Somers would have been familiar with mercantilist thought. Indeed, it was said that, "the merchants celebrated him as the only Lord Chancellor who had ever known any thing of trade or finance" (Weld 1848, p. 342). He supported Locke's commercial principles, and on this basis had supported him for appointment as a "Lord of Trade" (p. 342).

Somers would have also been familiar with Petty's work because of his involvement with the Royal Society, for which he served as president from 1698 to 1705 and actively attended its sessions. His predecessor Robert Southwell was the guardian of Petty's papers and was still an active member once Somers assumed the position. In his history of the Society, Weld says:

> An ardent lover of literature and science, he had, as a Fellow, long been in the habit of frequenting the Meetings ... he now regularly attended [after being relieved of the High Chancellorship], presiding over the Council and ordinary Meetings and doing all in his power to extend the reputation and usefulness of the Society. (p. 345)

Somers was familiar therefore with Petty's work and methods. A copy of Petty's *Quantulumunque Concerning Money* was in the Somers papers that Sir Walter Scott later included in *A Collection of Scarce and Valuable Tracts* from Somers' papers. In the same volume, Somers cites Petty's calculations in a tract on British trade with France, Spain, and Italy (p. 555). Given that Davenant knew Godolphin, it is likely that Somers did too. Further, he refers to Davenant and Petty in his *True Secret History* (1730) and Petty in *The Security of Englishmen's Lives* (1718).

Regardless of the political advantages of having Scotland being a part of a united country with England, Somers was also aware of its mercantilist value. In his work on the history of the kings and queens of England, he reflects on Edward III's peace negotiations with Robert the Bruce for Scotland's sovereignty, of which he clearly did not approve. For England's "irreparable loss" of the charter to the kingdom of Scotland and losses from the war, "in consideration of all of this King Bruce was to pay thirty thousand marks. A price too small in comparison of the value of what we parted with" (1730, p. 76). That Somers, who was both the commissioner who attended more meetings than any other and on the committee to calculate revenues and taxes related to England, attempted to quantify or make up for that loss through the way in which he crafted the articles can be seen in the examination in the remaining sections of this chapter and Chap. 5 (Minutes of the Commissioners 1707, p. 25).

4.2 The Drafting of the Treaty and the Articles as Structural Violence

When the English and Scottish commissioners met in April 1705, it was the English who dictated the terms of the treaty. This can be seen in the published minutes and in the eyewitness accounts left by John Clerk (1993) and George Lockhart (1714), who, he claims, besides the Archbishop of York were the only anti-Unionists among the commissioners. Although the Scots had come prepared with their own proposal for a federal union, which conceded on the issue of the Hanoverian succession in return for free trade, it was rejected without discussion and the English presented their own for a full incorporating union. Bishop Burnet says in his memoir that "the Scotch had got among them the notion of a federal union, like that of the United Provinces or of the cantons in Switzerland. But the English resolved to lose no time in the examining, or discussing of that project" for the main reason that as long as there were separate parliaments in each country, either one could break from the Union (p. 792).

According to Lockhart, the Earl of Seafield, who presented the Scottish proposal, did not fight for it and allowed that they would also consider an incorporating union. The only major complaint Seafield brought against the English proposal was that it contained too many new taxes and asked for abatements. This news caused some outcry in England as it was assumed that the English were being asked to pay higher taxes than those who would now be their countrymen. A lowering of the new taxes was rejected, but the English commissioners wrote in promises of economic development for fishing and manufacturing in Scotland. In addition, a one-time payment from England to Scotland called the Equivalent was established that was designed to compensate the Scottish people for the added burden of taxation, losses from reminting of the coinage, and losses to investors from the closure of the Company of Scotland. These all conferred seeming advantages to Scotland over England; but due to the nature of the negotiations this was not necessarily the case.

Defoe said that the mystery of the Union was that rather than the negotiating for the good of the future nation

> these gentlemen were for making bargains between the nations, not for bringing two great and mighty kingdoms into one vast body … The advocates of either people talked like counselors pleading for their clients, not like two friends striving … for the interest and engagement of the love of each other. (1799, p. 58)

Although Defoe is clear in his recollection that both sides fought for their positions, the commissioners did not enter negotiations as equals. Because of the threat that the Alien Act and military action could still take place, there was a power imbalance in the negotiations. The English commissioners rejected the initial proposals of their Scottish counterparts out of hand without discussion. So the process can be seen to be structurally violent in that the English had implicit veto power over the other side. It can also be seen that the articles themselves contain forms of structural violence, in some cases very subtle and in others more overt. Here I will explore the aspects of the articles and the debates over them in the negotiations in 1705 and in the last session of the Scottish Parliament in 1706 that demonstrate this argument.

4.2.1 The Debate in the Scottish Parliament

The final Scottish Parliament was called on October 3, 1706. Queensberry served as Lord Commissioner. Despite the unseasonably cold weather and rain, the event still "brought together an unprecedented Number of People of all Ranks, Sexes, Ages, and Persuasions, from all Corners of the Land, to Edinburgh" (Lockhart 1714, pp. 218–219). The traditional Riding of the Parliament through the streets was more impressive than in years past, according to our eyewitnesses.

From the outset, the session was rife with tension as to whether it was legal to hold a vote on the articles. Members of the Country and Cavalier parties, traditionally Jacobites and Episcopalians and the mainstay of the opposition, objected that not only had they not been able to consult with their constituents but also that the parliament had been authorized only to discuss, not vote on, the articles. Their spokesman, the Duke of Hamilton, attempted to halt the session because the ministers had been elected to discuss a union, not to "enact its own death, which the Articles of Union clearly prescribe" (Clerk 1993, p. 95). Fletcher's Squadrone Volante also sided with the Country party. The pro-Union Court party, those who supported the Hanoverian succession and many of whom had held offices with William or Anne, led by the Earl of Seafield, countered that Scotland was already dead but the Union would revive it (Clerk 1993, p. 96). Hamilton's motion to halt proceedings until protests were sent to Queen Anne failed by 64 votes, but his party succeeded in having both the articles and the proceedings published for the public (Clerk 1993, pp. 95–96; Lockhart 1714, pp. 219–222).

Popular sentiment, already strong against the Union, worsened once the full text of the articles was published. Lockhart reports that

> the Nation's Aversion to the Union increased; the Parliament Close, and the outer Parliament House, were crowded every Day when the Parliament was met, with an infinite Number of People, all exclaiming against the Union, and speaking very free Language concerning the Promoters of it. (p. 222)

Clerk concurs that "The buildings and streets around Parliament were thronged and there was every prospect of violence" (p. 97). Riots against the union on the night of October 23 caused Queensberry to issue a Proclamation Against Assemblies and to place guards in the Parliament House. Meanwhile, the English moved their troops closer to the border and had more ready to sail from Northern Ireland (Clerk 1993, pp. 103–104; Defoe 1799, p. 142; Lockhart 1714, pp. 225–227).

Public opposition was also shown formally in a number of addresses before the parliament, which are printed in Lockhart's history. The Address from the Majority of the Barons, Freeholders, Farmers, Heretors, and the Burghs states that the Union violated their traditional rights and asked that the treaty be rejected in favor of upholding the independence of the kingdom and its church. The Address from the Royal Borroughs in Relation to Trade protested the high tax rates in the treaty. They further protested that no consideration had been made for the differences in Scottish and English trade and thus should be subjected neither to the same laws as English commerce nor to the same parliament. A third address, from the Company of Scotland, opposed the dissolution of the company and the treaty's lack of security for Scottish merchants engaged in overseas trade.

Queensbury did not allow discussion on the addresses and moved the session to the debate and vote on the articles. The debates on the Union were lively, as can be seen in the eyewitness records, but shall not be fully recounted here. Instead, I will focus on the articles on economic issues and that created a particular political structure that gave England an advantage in legislating economic issues into the future.

In the first two articles, Scotland had to surrender the sovereignty fought for in the Act of Security. Article I of the Union called for the creation of one country and dissolved Scotland as an independent political unit. The debate in the Scottish Parliament centered on whether the ministers had the right to dissolve their legislative body according to the Scottish constitution. Dissolving the political identity of Scotland while the English were not required to do the same certainly gave the English an advantage.

The Hanoverian succession was settled in Article II. While the Scottish commissioners had written the Hanoverian succession into their original draft, this concession had multiple consequences for Scotland. With one monarch, Scotland and England's foreign policy decisions, and therefore international trade policy, would be the same, the problem the Act of Security sought to eliminate that was explored in Chap. 2. Although it ensured the Protestant succession, Article II also made impossible, without an overturning of the Union, a return to the throne of Scotland's traditional Stuart monarchs. Agreeing to settle the succession on Sophia, Electress of Hanover had required the removal of 51 persons directly from the line of succession. A joint monarch also meant the monarch would reside in London and, just as with the 1603 regal union, would likely favor English interests.

A further structural disadvantage was built into Article III, which created a united parliament that was to meet in London only. The new body drastically reduced the number of Scottish representatives, as stipulated in Article XXII. The Scottish Parliament itself was to be dissolved, but rather than a dissolution of the English Parliament or a loss of its representatives the Scottish ministers were to *join* the English. As opponents of Article III argued, this measure would deny Scotland any sovereignty and independence over its policy and its ecclesiastical and civil rights (Lockhart 1714, pp. 261–267). The ecclesiastical rights were later guaranteed in a separate article, but the parliament issue remained. In his opposition speech, Andrew Fletcher called again for federal union, as he had since the session of 1703. Given the imbalance of legislative power, he argued a full union was not possible. Fletcher clearly saw the structural violence inherent in Article III, stating that "what they offer is not union but dominion" (Clerk 1993, p. 127). With the parliament and the court situated in London, money would flow into the capital to the detriment of the country's commerce and Edinburgh's in particular. The pro-Unionist ministers did not have a direct answer to Fletcher's objections except that maintaining separate governments required by a federal union would invite war with England. The price of peace was thus Scotland's parliament.

Free trade and navigation were granted in Article IV. Although the majority of the arguments concerning the benefits to Scotland from the Union focused on the necessity of external trade for Scotland's prosperity, Article IV did not fully grant free trade. Scotland was to be allowed to trade with England, the colonies, and plantations, but this also opened Scottish markets to competition from more advanced English manufactured goods. As for access to trade with the East Indies, traders there were already supplied with the same goods Scotland produced more expensively and thus producers would not benefit. The other jarring condition of free trade was that the Company of Scotland was required to shut down but all English monopoly companies would stay intact. Additionally, Scotland would not be allowed to export raw wool because it would be injurious to English trade in wool, which meant the loss of a large portion of the Scottish general revenue (Clerk 1993, pp. 133–135). An address given by the Royal Commission of Trade of the Royal Burghs pointed to the same power imbalance as Fletcher had and argued that the conditions of Article IV would drive Scottish manufacturers out of business (Lockhart 1714, p. 268). Lockhart found it telling that those who were experts in trade were also opposed to the conditions in the articles.

John Dalrymple, the Earl of Stair, spokesman for the pro-Union side, argued that access to more markets was worth the risk and that Scottish workers and producers would simply have to become better to compete with their English counterparts. The access to ports would help the Scottish linen trade and the wool export ban would allow more inputs to stay at home and be made into other goods, he argued. Stair was willing to overlook the disadvantages of the article for what he thought it offered:

> Are you then willing to liberate yourselves and your descendants, to find a wider field for the exercise of virtue, open new avenues of trade, give skill and hard work better opportunities? All these lie within your reach. This article opens up a road which will carry this country to the heights it dreams of. (Clerk 1993, pp. 134–137)

Although Article IV allowed free trade, Article V ensured that any increase in Scottish trade had to benefit England. Article V required that any ships engaged in trade be registered in London, which was not the custom of Scottish merchants who had traditionally had ships built in or chartered from other countries (Defoe 1799, p. 49; Clerk 1993, p. 137). "The previous article gave us free trade," the opposition speech declared, "this one ensures we shall lack ships to carry it on … What is the value of trading privileges that we are prevented from using?" (Clerk 1993, p. 137).[1] The counterargument of the Court party was that the English were the best shipbuilders in the world, and so it would be best for the Scots to buy ships from them (p. 138). Scottish trade would presumably increase, but the costs of Scottish merchants and shipping would also increase while the English shipbuilding industry would be advantaged.

Uniformity of excises was required in Article VI. Scotland's excises were lower than England's and of course the English argument was that to allow them to remain the same would hurt England's trade. Similarly, raising them to the same level as in England was hurtful to Scottish trade, as argued by the opposition in the Scottish parliamentary debates. However, the Court party argued that the goods under consideration were mostly luxuries and thus the incidence would fall on the rich, to whom they would not pose an undue burden. The Earl of Stair also argued that higher taxes were simply Scotland's part of the Union to bear and would still have been required even in the case of a federal union (Clerk 1993, pp. 139–142). A committee was formed to determine the extent of the difference of English tax rates and found that they were "not much greater" than the Scottish (Clerk 1993, pp. 142–143). Before the article was passed, it was amended however so that there would be no additional duties on goods imported or exported to private individuals and that Scottish cattle sent to England after Union be exempt from export taxes. The equality of taxation ensured that there was a financial cost to the Scottish imposed by the Union. Rather than a reassessment of all taxation, the English tax rate was adopted.

Uniformity of taxation was also the subject of Articles VII (uniformity on all liquors) and VIII, which called for equal taxes on all imported liquors and salt, respectively. The liquor tax was opposed on the grounds that its burden fell unduly on the poor. The ale the poor drank in Scotland, for instance, would be taxed at the same rate as best ale consumed in England. After much debate, the article was approved with an amendment that the taxes were not to exceed the maximum amount the poor could bear.

There was also concern for the poor in the salt tax, as well as for the majority of Scots. Scotland used more salt than England. Salt was a necessity of the Scottish poor and the fishing industry. Salt was also a major

Scottish export and there was a fear that "by taxing it, the Dutch, who have no Duty upon Salt, can and will easily undersell them" (Lockhart 1714, p. 269). Article VII also imposed high duties upon the importation of tar, linseed, iron, and timber, which the English had in abundance but the Scots imported. Importation of English cloth and other goods was allowed, but the article disallowed the export of Scottish wool to England, which "did all stand in direct Opposition to Scotland's Welfare" (p. 269). After compensatory amendments were made to the article, including granting subsidies or "encouragements" to Scottish fish-exporters at the same rate as those granted to English fish-exporters, it was approved. Abatements were also negotiated until 1710 for some taxes on some excisable liquors, with the concern that they placed too heavy a burden on poorer household (Clerk 1993, pp. 145–147). Concerns about the salt tax caused serious debate in parliament, likely due to the potential loss of demand for domestic producers' products. Article VIII was not passed until amendments had been passed for the salt tax to be abated until 1714 and then instituted at a lower rate than originally proposed (Whately 1989, pp. 159–161).

Article IX called for Scotland's land tax to increase from £36,000 per year to £48,000, as determined without explanation by the English commissioners at the negotiations. England's land value was assessed at just over £1 million. The opposition argued that Scotland should not have to pay more than £36,000, but despite much debate the article was passed with no amendments.

Clerk says Articles X–XIII "offered little room for dispute and created the impression of a truce" (p. 147). These articles stated that Scotland would be taxed at a lower rate than the English on paper products, windows and lights, coal and cinders, and malt. Article XIV granted that no further duties would be applied to Scotland except for those agreed upon in the treaty—unless the monarch saw fit to do so after the union (Defoe 1799, pp. 52–53). These Articles passed with little debate.

Articles III and XXII on the new parliament were some of the most hotly contested of the treaty. It was not only the notion of a single parliament that was controversial, but also that Article XXII called for the new body to meet in London and a reduction of the number of Scottish ministers.[2] There were 239 representatives in the commons and 67 peers in the Scottish Parliament. Article XXII called for 45 members in the House of Commons, a revision upward from the negotiations that had called for 38, and 16 in the House of Lords. There was no plan for a similar reduction of representation of the English ministers, whose numbers would remain at 588 in the Commons and 156 in the House of Lords.

The opposition argued that the proposed representation was impracticable given the needs of the Scots. An anonymous pamphleteer, believed to be Andrew Fletcher of Saltoun, wrote that it was impossible that

> these separate distinct Interests and Establishments, can be regulated and supported by one Parliament… It is much easier to corrupt 45 Scots in London, than it is to corrupt 300 at Edinburgh, and besides, there will be no occasion of corrupting them, when the Case shall occur, of a difference betwixt the South-Britons and the North-Britons; for the Northern will be out-voted, without being corrupted … the Scots can be injured in an united Parliament with greater safety… Scots Members may dance round to all Eternity, in this Trap of their own making. (quoted in Dalrymple 1768, p. 68)

Checks could be placed on the power of the representatives in Edinburgh, but with the new parliament so far away there would be no local oversight to prevent the corruption of its members. Further, the English would be able to "injure the Scots in their trade" through such influence and "by laws passed in an English parliament" (p. 68).

Not only would Scottish concerns not be properly represented, the opposition argued, but also, being situated in London, the ministers would be too far removed from Scotland to be fully informed and up-to-date on Scottish concerns. Economically, sending the representatives to live in London would draw even more money and demand out of the country that otherwise would have stayed in Edinburgh (Clerk 1993, pp. 160–161). And yet, if they did not send the representatives to London, Scotland's affairs would be settled without Scottish input. Another loss to the Scottish people was their right to appeal in their parliament. The English did not have a similar law and so to allow the Scottish to keep theirs in the Union would be unfair, the English commissioners had argued.

The Earl of Stair countered that the reduction of ministers was actually a savings because the country would spend less money on its representation than otherwise. He excused the loss of the right of appeal on the same grounds as the commissioners had: such a right would be unfair to the English. However, he provided no justification for the reduction of parliamentary representation on its own merits. The English could not be expected to reduce any of their number, he argued, because they did not have to; they were dictating the terms of the treaty (pp. 161–164). This was a rare admission regarding the power imbalance that had been present since the negotiation of the treaty.

Indeed, one could not defend the reduction of Scottish representation if one is trying to make representation proportional to population. The Minutes of the Commissioners omit the discussion of how representation was decided and record only the outcome. Defoe (1799), who was privy to the conversations involved at the negotiation stage, claims that they were based initially on values determined under Cromwell's Commonwealth, but also says that "it is impossible to get the particular arguments used on both sides" (p. 106). The Scots had argued that these were arbitrary and that proportions should be set according to taxation per capita, but not the present tax rates as Scotland's tax burden would rise after the Union. The English agreed to reconsider the matter (p. 106).

Fortunately, Clerk, who was present at the negotiations, reports more details. The Scottish commissioners argued that the numbers should be based on population and the "national dignity" of each or to merge both extant parliaments (p. 86). The English replied that "it is natural justice that those who have money should have the spending of it," and argued that representation should be based on taxation, although they conceded that their own seats were not so distributed (p. 88). Reform would be more difficult than instituting the new rule for the addition of the Scottish ministers. When the Scottish argued that the basis for representation be the future tax revenue, which would be higher under the Union, the English response was that they were being compensated for increased taxes and English land tax revenues would still be higher (pp. 86–87). And that they were already making a sacrifice to their parliamentary tradition to allow the Scots to join them, "one of many inconveniences that we are forced to disregard to promote this island's welfare" (p. 87). Where the final numbers came from however is not explained, only that the final number was increased. In his memoir, Bishop Burnet claims that the numbers were more than fair to Scotland because, although it was to carry only a 40th of the public tax burden, it was to have 11% of the total seats in parliament (p. 799).

4.2.2 Protest

It is telling that when it was decided that there would be a walkout, it was on the grounds of the disadvantages in trade, taxation, and representation built into the articles. The author of the planned protest, the Duke of Hamilton, knew that Article XII in particular would be a barrier for many whose votes were still undecided.

The opposition's plan was to enter a motion to settle the Hanoverian succession but reject the rest of the treaty. Assuming the Court party would not approve this motion, Hamilton was to enter a protest on behalf of all opponents of the Union and then all such opponents would walk out of the parliament building. An official protest and a copy of the addresses against the Union heard in the parliament would be sent to Queen Anne. The actions were intended to show that the current treaty was against the will of the people and the parliament was acting with no authority (Lockhart 1714, pp. 293–295).

Although the draft of the protest was circulated by others, the author of the document was Lord Advocate Sir James Steuart, who

> tho' he could not be persuaded to speak and declare his Mind against the Union in the Parliaments, yet was heartily averse to it, and as soon as it became under serious Consideration, deserted the House, and could not be prevailed upon, either by the Threats or Cajoling of the Court to return and assist them in promoting it. (Lockhart 1714, pp. 295–296)

There is further corroboration for Advocate Steuart's feelings on the Union, as he made these known to the Earl of Mar, John Erskine, and the other commissioners. Mar writes to Seafield on September 22, 1706:

> Your lordship heard formerly that the Queen's Advocate did not like it [the Union], and nothwithstanding of all the Commissioners and the rest of the Queens servants can say to him, he continows of his own opinion, and argowd against it to us all together. (Erskine 1706, p. 175)

It will be recalled from Chap. 2 that Steuart also was the author of the passage in the Act of Security that closely tied the granting of trade and freedom from interference to the succession. Steuart's protest, reprinted in Lockhart, is worth reviewing at length because it reveals the issues of contention to be the same as have been discussed here regarding trade, representation, and taxation. The first section reiterates that parliament does not have the authority to lessen the number of their representatives or to strip voting privileges from the current peers, and notes that the House has ignored the addresses made by all of the estates. Steuart says that the Articles of Union are "manifestly tending to subvert that Original, Fundamental, and Indissolvable Constitution, by which the People of this Ancient Kingdom are joyned together in a Society amongst themselves" (Lockhart 1714, pp. 299–300). The second section is concerned with the movement of the capital to London and the English trade and regulations dictated by the treaty,

> as tending to drain this Nation of the far greater part of the product of the Customs and Excise which formerly remained at Home towards paying our own Ministry, and other necessary Charges of the Government, but must hence forward go out, seeing upon the event of this Union, our Government and Ministry must be translated forth of this Kingdom, as tending to ruin the Trade and Subjects of this Kingdom, by engaging them into insupportable Customs and Burdens upon Foreign Trade and Home Consumption, and by involving the Trade of Scotland, under the Regulations of the Trade of England, tho' the Funds, Export and Import, and the common Means of living in the South and North, are of such different Natures that the Regulations that are necessary in the South, will be ruinous to the Trade and Living in the North. (pp. 304–305)

Steuart concludes that the protestors will not stand for the dissolution of parliament or the rights that the representatives, burgesses, barons, and freeholders currently enjoy.

However, the protest failed due to Hamilton's lack of leadership. The protestors had agreed to walk before the vote on Article XXII, and many eminent citizens and gentlemen came to Edinburgh to escort the protestors out of the House. Hamilton failed to appear after succumbing to a convenient toothache, which may have been caused by a rumored threatening visit from Seafield the previous night. By the time a second speaker was found, many of the opposition had already left the House in frustration. Official protests were given by Lockhart and five others that the article violated the rights of the burghs; that barons and burgesses sat in Scotland as judges in civil and criminal cases but in England one could only go to Justice at the Bar of the House of Lords; that the English were not amending their constitution at all; that the Scottish ministers' votes would hold little weight; and that there had been not a single address in favor of the Union (L 326–331). The frustrated opposition believed the vote could not go forward with so many absent, but Queensbury saw this as the perfect opportunity to vote on the article without further complications and Article XXIII easily passed.

4.3 Advantages and Disadvantages

Throughout the Articles of Union, a pattern emerges of seeming freedom and privileges granted to Scotland but that are always counterbalanced by some extra cost, whether political or financial, explicit or implicit. A situation is created whereby England is never at a disadvantage but always maintains a surplus of benefits. Although, for instance, the English grant Scotland free trade, the Company of Scotland must close while the English East India Company (EIC) remained, so that whatever is lost in competition from Scottish merchants was gained in the continued dominance of the EIC. While there was to be a united parliament where Scottish ministers would have some say over matters pertaining to England, the representation is structured such that the Scottish ministers can never have a majority, and thus no deciding voice over the policy of England or their own. The shift of political capital in this arrangement is extreme.

The movement of the physical political capital of Scotland to London in the form of its representatives is also costly. The increases in taxation in Scotland are justified as a means of paying the increased costs of upkeep of Scotland or an extension of national defense to its borders. However, at the same time the English gain soldiers, finance, and material for their wars and their national defense.

The gain of trade is countered by increased customs and excise taxes. Any benefits of increased income for the Scottish are also countered by an increase in sales taxes on a number of goods. Benefit from an increase in exports is countered by an increase in customs duties. The Articles of Union were designed to give seeming advantages to Scotland while at the same time subtracting them through some other means. Although the English ministers did not write in explicit tax reductions for themselves, the customs and excise taxes of the Scots were to be applied to the English national debt. This extra source of payment meant that English taxpayers had potentially decreased their own tax burden for the debt into the future; it would now be partially paid by those for whom the debt had never been incurred.

Somers as the main architect of the Union was masterful in ensuring that the English attained their goals of security on the northern border, the Protestant succession, limitation of Scottish power in politics, limitation of Scottish influence over English policy just by brunt of numbers, and an extraction of payments and resources from Scotland, directly in the form of taxation and indirectly in the form of unbalanced terms of trade and the movement of peoples into English manufacturing and defense, in return for the opening of trade, that itself came with restrictions. The surplus of political, physical, and financial capital lay with England.

However, at the time some English critics assumed that by opening trade and allowing a temporary abatement of the tax increases in Scotland England had sacrificed too much. Burnet argues that the treaty was "so favourable to the Scotch nation," and that if not for the safety it supplied, it did not confer any favors on England (p. 799). Similar opinions among the English often considered not the disadvantages to Scotland embedded in the articles, but only the granting of freer trade, Scotland's lower public tax, and the payment of the Equivalent contained in Article XV.

The Equivalent was a highly controversial matter for supporters and critics of the Union. Another creation of the treaty negotiations, it bears the hallmarks of mercantilist thinking both in its uses and its construction and thus is deserving of examination in a separate chapter.

Notes

1. On Scottish producers who opposed free trade with England, see Whately (1989, pp. 157–165).
2. The representation of Scottish ministers in a united parliament was also a controversial point in proposals for union in 1670. The insistence of the Scottish Earl of Marchmont that Scotland maintain the full number of its current representatives in a united parliament was a major cause of English rejection of the legislation (Mason 2015). For more on the proposed union of 1670, see C. Jackson (2011).

References

Burnet, G. 1840. *Bishop Burnet's History of His Own Time*. Vol. II. London: William Smith.

Clerk, J. 1993. *History of the Union of Scotland and England*, trans. and ed. D. Duncan. Edinburgh: The Scottish History Society.

Dalrymple, J. 1768. *Memoir of Great Britain and Ireland*. London: T. Cadell and W. Strahan.

Defoe, D. 1706. *The Advantages of Scotland by an Incorporate Union with England*. Edinburgh.

———. 1799. *The History of the Union Between England and Scotland*. Dublin: John Exshaw.

Erskine, J. 1706. Letter to Lord Sidney Godolphin. September 22. In *Letters Relating to Scotland in the Reign of Queen Anne*, ed. J. Ogilvy. Edinburgh: Edinburgh University Press.

Jackson, C. 2011. The Anglo-Scottish Union Negotiations of 1670. In *Religion, Culture, and National Community in the 1670s*, ed. T. Clayton and T. Corns, 36–65. Cardiff: University of Wales Press.

Lockhart, G. 1714. *Memoirs Concerning the Affairs of Scotland from Queen Anne's Accession to the Throne to the Commencement of the Union*. London: Booksellers of London and Westminster.

Mason, R.A. 2015. Debating Britain in Seventeenth-Century Scotland: Multiple Monarchy and Scottish Sovereignty. *Journal of Scottish Historical Studies* 35 (1): 1–24.

The Minutes of the Proceedings of the Lords Commissioners for the Union. 1707. London: J. Tonson and T. Goodwin.

Petty, W. [1769] 1672. Political Anatomy. In *Tracts Chiefly Relating to Ireland*, 299–467. Dublin: Boulton Grierson.

Scott, W., ed. 1814. *A Collection of Scarce and Valuable Tracts*. Vol. 12. London: T. Cadell and W. Davies.

Somers, J. 1705. *An Essay Upon the Union of the Kingdoms of England and Scotland*. London.

———. 1718. *The Security of Englishmen's Lives*. London: J. Smith.

———. 1730. *The True Secret History of the Lives of All the Kings and Queens of England*, 2 vols. London: D. Browne.

Weld, C.R. 1848. *A History of the Royal Society, with Memoirs of the Presidents*. Vol. 1. London: John W. Parker.

Whately, C. 1989. Economic Causes and Consequences of the Union of 1707: A Survey. *Scottish Historical Review* 68 (186): 150–181.

5

Balancing Act: The Equivalent, Political Arithmetic, and Mercantilist Structural Violence

Abstract This chapter examines Article XV, on the Equivalent, in detail. Ostensibly a payment to Scotland in compensation for the losses incurred by the Union, the primary documents examined show that this was not the case. An examination of the calculation of the Equivalent demonstrates the influence of political arithmetic and the positive balance concept. Rather than compensation, it is argued that the Equivalent is a refund from Scotland to Scotland for increased taxes that financed England's pre-Union debts. Debate over the Equivalent in the Scottish Parliament and contemporary opinion is also discussed. Although seeming to be an advantage given to Scotland, the Equivalent is shown to be another instance of mercantilism where the English ministers built a structural advantage for their taxpayers into the reimbursement.

Keywords The Equivalent • Article XV • Union • Scotland • Debt • Surplus • Balance • Political arithmetic • Mercantilism • Company of Scotland • Taxation • Parliament • William Paterson • Calculation

A. Ramos, *Shifting Capital*, Palgrave Studies in the History of Economic Thought,
https://doi.org/10.1007/978-3-319-96403-4_5

Given the inequalities already built into the Union treaty, one is understandably led to ask how a majority of the parliamentarians present approved the Articles with so few amendments. One element that has been theorized to have swayed many was Article XV, which established the Equivalent as compensation from England to Scotland for losses incurred due to the Union. A committee selected by the parliaments of both countries calculated the payment to be £398,085 and 10 shillings, and disbursement of the fund was to be decided by the current Scottish Parliament. However, the opposition warned their countrymen not to be swayed by the financial enticement of the Equivalent, which they likened to the price to betray the country. The Duke of Atholl demanded of his fellows:

> Who have promised it? The English. Who are to pay it? A nation of debtors. And if they default, what recourse do we have against superiour numbers? (Clerk 1993, p. 150)

Seafield and the Court party did not answer this relevant point, but made their own, which was, plainly, that Scotland needed the immediate infusion of funds the payment would provide. On the surface the Equivalent seemed like fair restitution to Scotland for the added financial costs of the union, such as the recoinage of Scottish money into English pounds sterling, the increased excise taxes and customs imposed on Scotland in the treaty, and to compensate the investors of the Company of Scotland.

The investors of the company required compensation because Article XV also required the Company of Scotland to dissolve by 1708. The company's officers presented their case to parliament that dissolution would leave them no means to recoup their losses, and that in their absence Scottish trade overseas would have to be carried by hostile English merchant companies that could not serve Scottish trade as well as a Scottish company could (Clerk 1993, pp. 151–153). Unconvinced, the majority voted to dissolve the Company of Scotland and ordered the company to turn over their accounts. In the committee deliberations on the use of the Equivalent funds, it was decided that the company officers and shareholders would receive payments. The remainder of the Equivalent was set aside to assist the wool trade, encourage the fisheries, develop manufactures, and for other projects (p. 154).

Much has been written about the Equivalent. To some contemporary commentators it was seen as the decisive piece of the articles that convinced the Scottish ministers to pass the treaty. As David Nairne, the secretary to the Scottish commissioners and member of the committee that calculated the Equivalent, wrote, "It is not arithmetick only that can make a man understand the Equivalent" (1706, p. 307). While it has been characterized variously as a bribe, "the price of Scotland," and as a compensation for the losses of Darien, the Equivalent can also be seen as a very straightforward mercantilist arrangement calculated according to political arithmetic by which its "fairness" was determined by a balance of payments that depended on losses and gains from trade on both sides. The mercantilist logic and political arithmetic methodology used to calculate the payment are illustrative of the dominance, impact, and persuasiveness of the mercantilist worldview in the treaty proceedings and the passage of the articles.

5.1 The Creation of the Equivalent

Although the Equivalent itself seemed steeped in mystery to the general public of both countries, its origins were simple. In the early sessions of negotiations in May 1706, the Scottish commissioners demanded an "equivalent," a commonly used term at the time for compensation in any measure for losses incurred in political agreements, for the increased customs and excises on beer and ale and other goods, which had been raised to the same level as England's, that were imposed in the articles. Because the revenue from the increase was to be used to finance English war debt contracted before the Union, the English commissioners agreed to a one-time compensation of these taxes through 1710. It was agreed that the uses of the payment were to be determined by the Scottish Parliament.

A six-person committee was appointed with members from both sides to decide how to calculate the Equivalent. Members of the committee included William Paterson, John Clerk, the mathematician David Gregory, and David Nairne, the secretary for the Scottish commissioners. According to Clerk's *Memoirs*, the mathematics professor Gregory and Paterson of Darien fame were the chief calculators of the figures used to arrive at the Equivalent (p. 61).

The *Minutes of the Commissioners* relay the results of the Equivalent calculations, but do not provide an explanation for how the proportions of loss and compensation were determined. Derringer (2018) and Watt (2014), as well as a contemporary pamphlet attributed to Clerk (1706), who served on the committee that double-checked the figures of the calculation committee, provide more details on how the calculations were crafted. Instead of a calculation based on negotiation over the perceived costs of the Union, it was decided to base the compensation on the amount of England's current debts that the Scottish taxes would pay. Because England serviced its debt through a portion of its customs and excises, these data were the basis of the compensation.

A difficulty encountered by the calculators of the Equivalent was determining the present value of the future customs and excises Scotland was to pay. These would not be the same as the current amounts because they were set to increase after the Union was enacted and because it was assumed Scottish trade would increase and thus its tax burden would also increase. Increases in the customs and excises that were implemented to finance the war with France were set to expire at different times, with all increases from this source ceasing in 1710. Gregory and the committee then had to calculate the present value of the future customs and excises Scotland and England would pay, and then the proportion paid by each. The calculators used the historical ratio of Scottish to English tax payments on certain goods in order to determine the expected future tax payments of each country.

The current Scottish tax levels were calculated to be £30,000 for customs compared to England's £1.3 million. Thus, Scotland was assumed to pay 2.2% of England's debt service through customs and 2.4% through excises. Scotland's contribution to England's debt payment was then calculated through 1710 based upon these proportions. The amount of the Equivalent, £398,085 and 10 shillings, was the present value of the expected future debt payments, proxied by customs and excise at a discount rate of 6.5%.

As Derringer admits, there were analytical choices made in the construction of the Equivalent. The choice to consider only the customs and excise taxes, instead of the increase in all taxation or a comparison of all taxes, the use of compound interest at 6.5%, which was a suggestion of

Paterson that others disagreed with, and the use of current Scottish customs and excise rather than the higher levels they would rise to after the Union when the abatements Scotland received on some items expired in 1714, affected the amount of the payment. The use of customs rather than a comparison of all taxes caused the Equivalent to be higher than it would otherwise be, and the other three factors listed caused it to be lower than otherwise. There was also of course the assumption that the customs and excises under review would actually cease in 1710 and not have to continue or be levied in another form to continue to finance old war debt (pp. 100–101).

Therefore, both the construction of the Equivalent and the rhetoric surrounding the Equivalent, that it is a compensation to Scotland for multiple losses, places it in the realm of political arithmetic.

5.2 The Equivalent and Political Arithmetic

A reason for using political arithmetic, besides gathering data for political programs or the ends of the state, is that, as Petty envisioned it, numbers and data are disinterested. Therefore, rather than forwarding an argument about compensation that favored one party or one county over another, a mathematically calculated Equivalent seemed to show no partiality to one side or the other. Even the very name Equivalent indicated fairness and balance. However as with all data, the numbers can hide or reveal more of the story.

While these figures are based in facts, there is still a sense in which very deliberate choices regarding a political outcome were made, which puts the calculation into the realm of political arithmetic. Political arithmetic involves the creation of statistics that are dependent upon theoretical definitions in order to exist. As described by Poovey (1998), "These numbers … describe abstractions that have been brought into being by a method; this method in turn has been designed to create knowledge about something that exists only as an effect of the method—that is, as part of a theory" (p. 130). An example of this is Petty's valuations of the people of England and Ireland, where, for instance, adults are valued at twice the rate of children and men and women are equally valued (pp. 123–138). This was not based on reality but on an abstraction from the values Petty established that equalized income to expenditure in the aggregate and assumed that these would be the same for individuals. According to his own definitions Petty's calculations are therefore correct. But Petty's methods highlight the assumptions one necessarily makes when creating "impartial" numbers. The Equivalent is a perfect example of political arithmetic of this kind. Compensatory "Equivalents" had been used in political negotiations before but never for the matter of compensating a country for its losses from a union, and more precisely for payments it made for debt it did not owe. These required new definitions. While the calculations that went into its construction are precise, they are based on a number of assumptions and definitions that were decided upon by committee both trying to determine how much Scotland would be compensated for its part of England's debt and its losses from joining the Union and trying to attain a particular political purpose.

According to the Minutes, the English commissioners agreed to the Equivalent because they were "extremely desirous to bring the Treaty to a speedy conclusion" and were willing to gain Scottish acquiescence by this means (p. 176). Thus, the English made use of calculation and the Equivalent in order to bring about their desired political ends. This is not to say that the numbers were wrong, because they were according to their own definitions correct, but simply that economic calculations had been put at the service of political calculus. Defoe concurs that without the Equivalent "it had been impossible to bring this Union to a Conclusion" (1709, p. 95).

From a political arithmetic standpoint, the Equivalent is a necessary by-product of the transmutation of Scotland into part of Great Britain. The Equivalent was a discounted cash flow of Scotland's projected increased customs and excises due to standardization of these taxes and increased trade from the Union. There are two ways in which the use of this metric can be interpreted. One is that the value of joining the Union, or the price exacted for free trade, was equated to what the Scots would gain through free trade. The other interpretation, if one sees this as a payment for Scotland's sovereignty, is that the price of Scotland was the extra revenue they would gain from free trade. Previous commentary on the Equivalent has said it was a bribe or simply a compensatory payment for the losses of Darien. However, from a political arithmetic perspective, other interpretations come to light. If one wanted to see it as a price paid by England for their security, the purchase price of Scotland is Scotland's gains from trade. In this the Equivalent is a mercantilist victory for the English commercial state, just as much as the Union is for the English political-military state. That the taxes that are the foundation of the Equivalent were made equal to England's debt payments for their war finance is merely mercantilist accounting. Analogous to the concept of foreign-paid income, the burden of payment for foreign wars is placed partially on those from another country and on those who are buying products from abroad.

5.3 Perceptions of the Equivalent

Although it was a payment demanded by the Scottish commissioners, the process of creating the Equivalent can however be viewed as a form of structural violence, albeit one that has been obscured in a payment. Both the conditions in which the Equivalent were constructed and those that it enforced entailed restriction of the Scots. The Equivalent itself was among other things, a gag in the form of a payment as it was expected that the Scottish ministers would not protest the terms of the treaty if they received this payment.

George Savile, the Marquess of Halifax, one of the Scottish commissioners at the treaty negotiations, observed this as well. In his *Anatomy of an Equivalent* (1706), he explains the Equivalent and its context in a way in which his contemporaries would have understood and that modern analysts may have overlooked. When the Scottish commissioners and public showed resistance to the terms of Union, Halifax says, the English commissioners' response was to put before them a proposal where "instead of an absolute quitting of our TRADE, LIBERTY, LAWS, and all that is valuable upon uncertain conditions"; the English commissioners' response was akin to saying, "if you Scots acquiesce in the articles proposed, you shall sometime or other have as good a thing for them." Halifax continues, "This … fashionable word is now called an Equivalent" (p. 1).

He finds the word not only distasteful but somewhat scandalous: "It is transmitted hither from France," where the king of France "promises largely and performs as much as he pleases" (p. 2). The true scandal of the word is not that it is French but *of the use of the French king's power* in bestowing an equivalent:

> Princes and potentates enjoys and prescribes things by strength and power to supply the want of arguments ... the weak are never thought to have an ill bargain ... So that the first quality of an Equivalent, must be that the parties to whom an Equivalent is proposed must have power to make his claim good, for without force persuasions will avail little. (p. 2)

There are two senses in which Halifax could be describing the power imbalance and the Equivalent: either that the English must be able and willing to use force to impose their bargain on the other party in order to avoid any protest to it or that the party being imposed upon, Scotland, must have some power in order to press its claim to a compensation. However, the context of the rest of the document implies that his meaning is the former rather than the latter. The English had the power of military invasion and economic threat of the Alien Act behind them to ensure that the Equivalent is accepted as a fair bargain whether it actually was or not.

The second quality of an Equivalent to those who must accept it, he says, is that the bargain is not fair "except the thing being offered is better in value than the thing demanded. There must be allowance for moving what is fixed, and there must be something that may be a justification for changing" (p. 2). Thirdly, both parties must be able to consent and to withdraw consent. Halifax specifies that it is not only equal terms that are required "but fair ones in the matter too" (p. 2). If anger "or open threatening" is a response to a refusal of a bargain, then it becomes "more like a breach of the peace than the making of a bargain" (p. 2).

Fourthly, he speaks of violence. Open physical violence obviously ends all contracts. However, he then describes a situation that is structurally violent: "Besides open violence, there is a secret one which may bribe and prepossess a great many of the representatives of a people ... that infects, poisons and corrupts the foundation of public security," and that is one created through biased legislation (p. 2).

The Scots had no option in the negotiations to reject the articles, which made it spurious legislation at best, according to Halifax. The lack of provision for resistance to the treaty or some of its terms was itself a very subtle form of violence by the English commissioners against the Scots. The acceptance of the payment of the Equivalent that benefitted the Scottish commissioners but not necessarily Scotland as a whole was another form of violence of the Scottish against themselves and their national self-interest.

If the treaty were sound, there would be no need to enforce it with threats of violence, structural or otherwise: "It is not only unnecessary, but unnatural too, to persuade with violence, what it is folly to refuse; to push men with eagerness into a good bargain for themselves" (pp. 3–4).

He returns again to the problem of force and imbalance of outcomes in such a case:

> There can be no dealing where one side assumeth a privilege to impose, so as to make an offer, and not bear the examination of it, this is giving judgment, not making a bargain ... if there should be a possibility that one of the parties be ruined by accepting, and the other only disappointed by his refusing; the consequences are so extremely unequal, that it is not imaginable a man should take that for an Equivalent, which hath such a fatal possibility at the end of it. (p. 4)

He also argues that if there is any suspicion or questionable aspects of any of the instruments of a treaty, it renders the entire treaty suspicious. The lack of a penalty or guarantee of the Equivalent's disbursement rendered the contract a bad bargain. Additionally, there was no stricture in the articles to prevent a new parliament of Great Britain from repealing parts of it or changing the contract. In addition to the several elements of structural violence in the Equivalent, Halifax reminds the reader too of the death the Scottish ministers are inflicting on Scotland itself in acceptance of the treaty. Demurring from any aspect of the treaty allowed the "Southern Britains for confiscation and conquest: By this voluntary surrender, we may happen to incur ... self murder" (p. 6). Halifax clearly believes in maintaining balances but he looks beyond the numbers to the structure of the payment and the structure of its logic relative to the entire treaty.

John Clerk, who also served on the committee that calculated the Equivalent, holds the opposite view of the Marquess of Halifax. Clerk explains in *Essay upon the Fifteenth Article* the fairness of the payment and why the Scots should not object to it. Consciously or not, he uses an array of mercantilist thinking regarding balances and maintaining "justness" thereby.

The reason for the Equivalent, Clerk argues, is because Scotland's excises and customs on all goods are going to rise to bring equality of taxation across Britain. He justifies this as a necessity for free trade because if their customs remained the same, "the Merchants residing in Scotland would be put in a Condition to ruin the whole trade of England" (p. 4). Excises also had to be equal because otherwise the lower costs of living in Scotland would allow them to "undersell" their neighbors. The reason the customs and excises figures were chosen as the proxy for Scotland's payment of England's debts was because England currently used part of these taxes to pay their national debt. Because the Equivalent would be paid to Scotland shortly after the implementation of the Union, Clerk argues that the Scottish people are not actually paying any part of England's debt. All Scottish customs and excises after the Union would be used to pay Scotland's own debts as part of Britain, and any other revenue would be used for payments the current parliament chose (p. 5).

Furthermore, the payment, Clerk asserts, allows Scotland to have an immediate fund the country can use for improvement and to better engage in the trade with England and the plantations that the treaty makes available (p. 6). If the customs and duties the Scottish have to pay after the Union increased as the customs and excises of England increase over the seven years because of continued payment of debts, the Scots would be able to use that money as they saw fit for the improvement of the economy. Clerk concludes: "In effect all these burdens will signify no more, than if we had taxed ourselves in sums of money, to be raised annually for the improvement of Scotland" (p. 7).

However, although he has stated that the customs duties are payments from Scotland to Scotland, he characterizes the Equivalent as a loan: "tis a very necessary loan of money, suitable to the poverty of this country, and the indispensible want of stocks we ly under, for enabling us to reach the full advantage of the communication of trade" (p. 27). In the very next sentence he changes his view, saying that because the money comes from customs and excises due to the Queen, she bestows the money to Scotland in the Equivalent (p. 27). So rather than seeing the funds as a payment from themselves, it becomes a grant to the country.

Other commenters focused on the imbalance of outcomes accepted in the treaty that were far from being equivalent. The merchant William Black (1706) wrote in a response to London merchants, who claimed Scotland had gained an advantage, that "the barren and empty name of a communication of trade, is not a sufficient Equivalent for our Sovereignty, Independency, and Laws" (p. 5). He asserts that currently Scotland enjoyed free trade with almost every country in Europe and that afterward their trade would be "circumscribed to particular Countries" or they would be forced to trade at a disadvantage (p. 5). The gains from the trade of the Union were not being measured by the Scottish people in simply economic terms, and nor were they being measured only as such by the English public either.

Indeed an anonymous member of the English public understood mercantilist thought and felt that the burdens of the Union were not being fairly meted out to those who benefitted most from it. In *An Essay upon the Equivalent*, the author questions why the English public should have to pay the Equivalent and proposes instead that the East India Company ought to make the payment. The company, the author reasons, is the entity that will benefit the most from the opening of trade. Scotland would increase its consumption of East Indian goods and thus cause profit to accrue to the monopoly. It is clear, the author claims, "that the monopoly, the ingrossment and violence of this company is greater than ever was under the charter of the Old" due to its recent seizure of ships that were bound for the East Indies but had not yet made it there. The company would also, the author argues, gain from absorbing the capital of the Company of Scotland and thus further consolidate its power (1706, pp. 1–3).

Defoe says that in the treaty negotiations the Scottish commissioners protested the Equivalent on the grounds that it was "a national satisfaction indeed, but not a personal; that it could not relieve the particular people it oppressed, no, nor make good the particular trade it would injure" and so rather than having an equivalent argued that the taxes on liquor and malt not be raised (1786, p. 141). These overtures were rejected on the basis that uneven duties would be hurtful to England's economy. Regardless, it is interesting to note that the commissioners perceived an injustice in the Equivalent but later voted for it, with the exception of Lockhart. His explanation is that the Scottish Parliament had decided that part of it would compensate shareholders of Darien and that many of the voting ministers stood to gain back some part of their investments. Analysis of voting patterns and compensation is somewhat inconclusive without further evidence. A strong correlation between voting patterns and compensation from the Equivalent can be seen in Shaw's analysis, wherein 69% of the Company of Scotland compensation went to members of parliament who voted for union (1999, pp. 4–5), but MacInnes makes the opposite case since only 42.7% of the voting members had a claim to compensation from the Company of Scotland (pp. 306–308). Of course, the articles could not have passed without those 42.7%.

5.4 Counting the Costs: A Mercantilist Analysis of the Equivalent

Whether one sees the Equivalent as a loan or a grant alters one's view of whether Scotland is a net gainer or loser from the payment. *An Essay upon the Equivalent* (1706) characterized it as a loan rather than a grant, in which case the English would be paid back with interest for debts they had incurred from which the Scottish did not benefit. William Black's essay *Some Considerations in Relation to Trade* treats the Equivalent in the same manner but with a more jarring conclusion: accounting for interest payments, Scotland was shown to overpay for the Equivalent as the amount received by the country over 11 years would be less than it was estimated to pay in customs and excise over the same period. Thus, there was a way in which the Equivalent could be interpreted in which the payment is actually a benefit in England's favor. Derringer shows that the calculations in the pamphlet rely on simple rather than compound interest to arrive at the conclusion. However, the perspective of the essay's author, to view the Equivalent from a creditor/debtor perspective, demonstrates the different ways in which the public interpreted the concept of the Equivalent.

Derringer observes that the Equivalent brought questions involving the relationship between present and future, not only in terms of the present valuation of funds to be paid in the future, but in terms of promises (p. 84). Acceptance of the values of the Equivalent meant the current population accepted a payment in exchange for future tax payments yet to made, whose value could ultimately not be known because the rate of taxation could rise or fall. However, the same is true of the Union itself: the present ministers made decisions that were binding on future generations politically and economically. Those who were accepting of the Equivalent felt it was proper compensation for the losses of the past. However, for those opposed it made no compensation for the losses of the future. The concessions made by the Scottish in exchange for free trade carried a high opportunity cost that could not be quantified. The balance of costs and payments thinking can still be seen in both groups.

What has been overlooked however is that the Equivalent cannot truly be seen as the price of Scotland because it was not an extra payment to them for the Union. Rather it was a means of maintaining a zero balance on England's debts. Any amount of their new taxes over this compensation would return to them. As Clerk observed, the Equivalent was essentially a payment from Scotland back to Scotland. Although in the sense of getting the initial portion of the payment back at once, Scotland had not an advantage but a short-term benefit that could be reinvested in the country, but in return England eliminated its potential trading company competitor and had a new source of funds for public debt from future Scottish excises after the Union.

The fund therefore was in reality neither a grant nor a loan but a refund of the future customs and excises that would go toward paying England's debt. Because it was a refund of money that the Scottish importers and consumers would pay in the future, it was a transfer of money from themselves to themselves. There was no gain, except in terms of time, of having a fund of cash on hand immediately.

Another function of the Equivalent, although in name it balanced out the Scots' losses, is to balance the perceived expected lost trade advantages of the English immediately after Union. The Scots were assumed to be net gainers from the Union because of the increase in trade that they were to have with England and the plantations. It was known that they had a lower cost of production simply due to being at a lower level of economic growth and development, on average, compared to England. Therefore, the English sought in the Treaty negotiations to protect themselves against competition from lower-priced Scottish goods that were presumed to be able to freely be imported into England after the Union. Therefore, the Scots could not escape the imposition of higher taxes on certain goods after a period of seven years.

During the seven-year grace period, Scotland had a small chance to be net gainers in trade vis-à-vis the English due to their lower costs of production and lower taxes. Therefore, the English sought a bulwark to protect their balance of trade. Scotland was also allowed a grace period of payments on the interest of the English debt. Despite appearances this did not amount to a gain either in reality or on paper. The calculation of the debt payments by the Equivalent commission was made equal to the customs and excise payments. Why was it done this way? Clerk, one of the commissioners on this committee, admits that there is no logical reason to equate these payments except that the English made payments on the national debt from their customs and excise revenue. Scotland's payments on the debt in the future would also come from any customs and excise revenues above its pre-Union levels. Thus, any increase in revenue for the Scottish state would not go to the Scottish state but to debt service for Great Britain, the majority of which debt was accrued before the Union. Another spurious factor in the calculation of the treaty was the payment of the Equivalent. It was in fact to come from the Scots themselves rather than from England.

Clerk admits this in his declamation against the protests that the English would never pay the bill. He argues that in reality there will be no coin or bill that comes from London to be disbursed among the Scots but that the money will simply be transferred from Scotland's new customs and excise revenue in the time period of the tax freeze to the Scottish people. Because of the structure of the agreement on the Equivalent, it is true that it is essentially a payment from Scotland to itself.

The English commissioners would see such a construct as fair because it meant that Scotland would not gain from the Union at England's expense. On the net the English would be gainers because they would increase their trade with Scotland and not have to change their tax and trade structures. In addition, they would gain new sources of paying down their national debt without having to pay out to compensate the Scots. At the same time, they eliminated a potentially large defensive military expenditure should they have gone to war to force Scotland's acquiescence. From a mercantilist standpoint this is an excellent outcome.

If one believes the total wealth of the world is fixed and that there can only be one winner and one loser in any two-sided transaction, then the construction of the treaty's terms and the Equivalent make perfect sense. The use of numbers also made the Equivalent seem like a sensible figure if one did not look too closely into the numbers. It is through political arithmetic that the Equivalent came to be close to the amount lost to the subscribers of the Darien venture. Poovey (1998) and Spence (2010) each characterize political arithmetic as the use of mathematics and statistics to advance a particular political agenda and that political arithmetic certainly seems to have been used this way in 1706. The political agenda of the English and some of the Scottish MPs was to create the Union, despite popular opinion or the benefit or cost of the project to either side. Mercantilist thinking and calculation helped to bring this agenda to fruition in a way that economically benefitted one side more than the other. The Equivalent achieved this by preventing the Scottish from being true gainers from the initial opening of trade. Any excess customs revenue would be tied up in the payment of the Equivalent. Any excess customs revenue after that would go to payment of the national debt, and Scottish taxes would rise on other goods after anyway. On net, the agreements built into the Articles of Union were mercantilist because they meant that Scotland would not see a net gain from the increase of trade.

Was the Equivalent a "swinging bribe" as Lockhart describes it (212)? Perhaps. In May 1707, Henry Maule wrote from Edinburgh to the Earl of Mar that, "the Equivalent is mightily longed for here ... for many an honest gentleman's credit depends upon it at the term" (p. 392). Regardless, it was also a clever instrument to attain mercantilist ends.

While disguised as compensation to Scotland, it was actually compensation to England for any losses they might incur from the loosening of trade restrictions on Scotland and the perceived unfairness that the Scots had a grace period from the increase in excises on the several items in Article VIII while the English did not. This makes sense only if one sees the world in mercantilist terms and makes effort to align one's calculations with a mercantilist political agenda. The Equivalent is likely also why the mercantilist Scottish MPs who were in favor of Union thought the treaty was not only fair but also that the Equivalent favored Scotland. Clerk could see through it to an extent because he had been present at the calculation discussions, but he still found a way to justify the committee's conclusions and the treaty through mercantilist logic.

5.5 Uncompensated

J.G. Pittendrigh (2007) characterizes the Equivalent as "an exercise in financial illusion" (p. 73). He means this though not in the sense that its calculation was erroneous but that it was simply insufficient to meet the losses it was claimed to cover. The capitalized value of the national debt that Scotland would be servicing came to the entire amount of the Equivalent. What was not covered was the cost of reminting the coinage, arrears of payments owed to government workers, and the Darien shareholders. Pittendrigh calculates that the sum was £300,000 short of its intended uses. The funds mentioned by Clerk to improve the fishery and manufactures was to come from any further increases in Scottish excises and customs from the expected increase in revenue from post-Union trade, not from the original payment itself (pp. 70–74).

Of course, the error in Pittendrigh's otherwise persuasive analysis is to assume the Equivalent was ever intended as a real compensation for Scotland's losses. The numbers used to calculate the Equivalent were neither fabricated nor an attempt to fool the public but rather an earnest effort to quantify what Scotland should be paid for financing England's debt and whatever other losses for which the Scottish committee earmarked the funds. However, of course the difficulty arises in the transmutation as it were of Scotland's losses into a financial recompense. Political arithmetic attempts to do so and mercantilism, or, more precisely, the mercantilist ideals that animated the entire sequence of events that led Scotland to accept this version of the Articles in the first place, created the necessity of doing so.

There were some things that the Equivalent, despite the language of Article XV, did not compensate. The Reverend Robert Wylie (1706) questioned, "How can the English ever give unto the Scots an Equivalent for their Resign'd Sovereignty?" (p. 6). Similarly, Lockhart writes, if Scotland was to have to an Equivalent for its losses due to the Union, "such particulars as redounded to England's advantage, where was the Equivalent for her Sovereignty, the removal of her parliaments and seat of government, which kept the Great Ones and consequently the money at home" (p. 271). It was not compensated by trade, which he says was against Scotland's interest in its particulars except for trade to the plantations. "And where was the Equivalent for the dissolution of the Scots African Companies?" Wylie asks when no recompense was made for the loss of the Darien colony and the abuse he said they suffered at the hands of the English (p. 272). Lockhart concedes that part of the Equivalent was used to pay the shareholders of the company but he correctly notes that the Scots had paid for the company themselves because "the Fund from which this sum had its rise did flow from Scotland" (p. 272). He calls the payment to the shareholders a bribe to close the company and identifies the transaction as essentially a gift to the East and West Indian Companies, which now had no Scottish competitors for their monopolies.

An episode at the drafting stage is very revelatory of how the English commissioners viewed the Equivalent. The Scottish Commissioners lobbied for the continuation of the rights of the Company of Scotland, but also fatally conceded that "if the privileges of that Company be judged inconvenient for the trade of the united kingdom, that the private rights of the said Company in Scotland be purchased from the said proprietors" (Defoe 1799, p. 176). In this they at least attained some payment for giving up the Company. However, this means that Lockhart is correct and compensation was not paid either for the loss of the future trade of the company or for the past losses of the shareholders. Although of course better than nothing, this was not a surplus payment to the people of Scotland overall because they had already previously paid for the shares of the company. Rather, despite the rhetoric surrounding it, the Equivalent was a payment to purchase the rights of the Company. Scotland lost future privileges from its Company, while the East India Company only strengthened its dominance.

Even if just considering items for which a financial cost could be calculated, in reality the Equivalent left Scotland at a loss. While they were refunded for their expected, but not actual, payments for England's debt service, they were not compensated for the other items that were listed in the article. The Equivalent was equal to their debt service, but once received that money was used to pay the Darien shareholders and other expenses. If there was an increase in Scotland's revenues from trade beyond their own debt obligations, they would be paying to themselves the payments that would otherwise go to England's debt service.

In addition to the conceptual and arithmetical challenges of the Equivalent, in reality Article XV's promised payment was only partially made. The payment arrived from England on August 5, 1707. According to James Ogilvy, the Earl of Seafield, the payment was "satisfying to all excepting the Jacobites and such as are foolish as to desire the Union to be overturned" and yet he reported that "stones were thrown" at the arrival of the carts bearing the payment (1707, p. 411). Its form was controversial with £100,000 in bullion and the remainder in notes of exchange. The notes were exchangeable for gold in England, but not in Scotland. Given this and that England had had to borrow money to send the bullion, there was immediate suspicion that the rest of the Equivalent would not be paid. The majority of the £100,000 and the rest of the payment went to the shareholders of the Company of Scotland. Others who were owed payment had to wait longer to receive their benefits, and in many cases sold their notes rather than continue to wait for their payment (Watt 2014, p. 241). According to Pittendrigh, the debentures were finally redeemed in 1850, which meant England had received a £248,000 interest-free loan for 143 years (p. 76).

The Equivalent paper debentures did eventually boost Scottish financial capital, but likely not in the way that Scottish supporters of the Equivalent had foreseen. When it was seen that the paper notes were unlikely to be redeemed for their full cash value, a market opened to buy and sell the notes. A group of note holders incorporated as the Equivalent company in 1724 and in 1727 were chartered by parliament to form a bank, which eventually became the Royal Bank of Scotland (Derringer, p. 116).

References

An Essay Upon the Equivalent. In a Letter to a Friend. 1706. Edinburgh.

Black, W. 1706. *Some Considerations in Relation to Trade*. Edinburgh.

Clerk, J. 1706. *An Essay Upon the Fifteenth Article of the Treaty of Union.* Edinburgh.

———. 1892. *Memoirs of the Life of Sir John Clerk of Pennicuik*, ed. J. Gray. Edinburgh: T. and A. Constable for the Scottish History Society.

———. 1993. *History of the Union of Scotland and England*, trans. and ed. D. Duncan. Edinburgh: The Scottish History Society.

Defoe, D. 1709. *The History of the Union of Great Britain*. Edinburgh: Andrew Anderson.

———. 1786. *The History of the Union Between England and Scotland with a Collection of Original Papers Relating Thereto*. London: John Stockdale.

———. 1799. *The History of the Union Between England and Scotland.* Dublin: John Exshaw.

Derringer, W. 2018. *Calculated Values: Finance, Politics, and the Quantitative Age*. Cambridge: Harvard University Press.

Halifax, Marquess of. 1706. *The Anatomy of an Equivalent*. Edinburgh.

Lockhart, G. 1714. *Memoirs Concerning the Affairs of Scotland from Queen Anne's Accession to the Throne to the Commencement of the Union*. London: Booksellers of London and Westminster.

MacInnes, A. 2007. *Union and Empire: The Making of the United Kingdom in 1707*. Cambridge: Cambridge University Press.

Maule, H. [1707] 1904. Letter to the Earl of Mar, May 13, 1707. In *Report on the Manuscripts of the Earl of Mar and Kellie*, ed. Historical Manuscripts Commission, 392. London: HMS Office.

The Minutes of the Proceedings of the Lords Commissioners for the Union. 1707. London: J. Tonson and T. Goodwin.

Nairne, Sir D. [1706] 1904. Letter to the Earl of Mar, Nov. 1, 1706. In *Report on the Manuscripts of the Earl of Mar and Kellie*, ed. HMC, 306–308. London: HMS Office.

Ogilvy, J. [1707] 1904. Letter to the Ear of Mar, August 5, 1707. In *Report on the Manuscripts of the Earl of Mar and Kellie*, ed. HMC, 411. London: HMS Office.

Pittendrigh, J.G. 2007. The Equivalent. In *The Union: How and Why?* ed. Henderson Scott, 69–78. Edinburgh: The Saltire Society.

Poovey, M. 1998. *A History of the Modern Fact*. Chicago: University of Chicago Press.

Shaw, J.S. 1999. *The Political History of Eighteenth-Century Scotland*. London: Palgrave.

Spence, C. 2010. Accounting for the Dissolution of a Nation State: Scotland and the Treaty of Union. *Accounting, Organizations, and Society* 35 (3): 377–392. https://doi.org/10.1016/j.aos.2009.09.005.

Watt, D. 2014. *The Price of Scotland: Darien, Union, and the Wealth of Nations*. Edinburgh: Luath Press Ltd.

Wylie, Robert. 1706. *A Letter Concerning the Union*. Edinburgh: Eighteenth-Century Collections Online, Gale, University of Dallas. Accessed 21 June 2018.

6

Shifting Capital

Abstract This chapter assesses the outcomes of the Union from the articles. It examines the trade advantages Scotland gained, the Equivalent, and the temporary exemptions from certain taxes. However, it draws attention to what was given up in exchange: the Scottish Parliament, the capital, and the Company of Scotland. In gaining a permanent majority in parliament, the closure of the East India Company's rival, and another source of capital and debt service, the chapter argues that England emerged the true winner of the positive surplus battle, from a mercantilist perspective. It examines the different forms of capital that were at stake in the Union decision, physical and financial, and concludes with a discussion of how Scotland's human capital remained intact due to its social institutions.

Keywords Political capital • Capital • Social capital • Financial capital • Human capital • Structural violence • Trade • Taxation • Act of Union • Scotland • England • Equivalent • Institutions • Mercantilism

A. Ramos, *Shifting Capital*, Palgrave Studies in the History of Economic Thought,
https://doi.org/10.1007/978-3-319-96403-4_6

In the final parliamentary session, members of the Country party made several speeches against the Union. "We are the servants of the state," one of the speeches said, "not its masters; fathers and guardians, not tyrants or traitors" (Clerk 1993, p. 170). The speaker likened the ending of the nation's sovereignty to a betrayal of the nation, and declared that by signing the Union treaty against the people's will "what you are doing is to turn loyal subjects into disaffected rebels" (p. 170). Certainly the first half of the eighteenth century was to see more than one Jacobite rising that seemed to make these words prophetic.

The pro-Unionists responded with a reminder that Scotland's glory had long since faded with the regal union, and that now trade was more valuable than sovereignty. However, in the end there was an open admission by the Court party that the union had been forced and the terms of the treaty were unbalanced, but that such concessions were necessary for Scotland's survival. The final speech by the pro-Unionists stated that it was England's "policy either to destroy us or to force us into union on well-defined terms. Choose then the role that Nature herself dictates to us" (Clerk 1993, pp. 173–174). The majority chose Union.

The articles were approved on January 16, 1707. Upon this news the English Parliament convened and quickly gave their approval to the articles on March 25, "a handsome new year's gift to that kingdom," as Lockhart groused (1714, p. 340). The Union was enacted on May 1, 1707. It was met with much celebration in England, as described in the Introduction, and with much more subdued temperament in Scotland. There was a sense in which the public seemed to know that the balance of benefits from the Union was not in Scotland's favor.

It has been the contention throughout this book that the balance concept pervaded thinking not only on economic matters but also on political ones. As Pocock (1975) says:

> an entity known as Trade entered the language of politics, and became something which no orator, pamphleteer, or theorist could afford to neglect and which, in an era of war, was intimately connected with the concepts of external relations and national power. (p. 425)

The positive balance model was at play not only in the negotiation of the Union but also persisted in economic policy after it, both in relation to Scotland and to Britain's post-Union external trade. Defoe said that the "great mystery of the Union" was that each side in the negotiations sought for advantages to their own nation and "never looked beyond the present state; never considered the conjunct capacity of the nations" (1799, p. 59). However, the mercantilist thought process that drove the creation of the Union was neither mysterious nor transitory and persisted beyond ratification of the Articles.

In the very short period between ratification and implementation of the Union, Scottish merchants attempted to gain an advantage by importing goods from their non-English trading partners at current low customs rates in order to export them to England customs-free after the Union. Another Scottish merchant scheme was the importation of tobacco from England before May 1 for export to Continent after May 1 to earn drawbacks on the customs paid. When Robert Harley and other English ministers became aware of these transactions, Harley attempted to pass legislation to thwart the merchants' profits. Harley wanted the English Parliament to pass measures that any Scottish goods purchased from the Continent before the Union went into effect were subject to standard duties, and that reexports of goods that had been acquired since February were banned after May 1. Therefore the immediate benefits the Scots received from gaining trade with their southern neighbors would be erased by the negation of the drawbacks imposed by the English measures. Counterprotests and lobbying by the Scottish ministers in London and Sir David Nairn, now the undersecretary for Scottish affairs at court, asserted that such measures were a violation of the Union treaty.

The loss to the Scottish traders was assessed to be approximately £300,000, or the positive in the balance of trade that the country would have attained shortly after the Union. This number is of course also very close to the Equivalent payment, which had raised some controversy in England where some saw it as a loss of the English funds rather than a reimbursement of Scottish taxes. Whether because it was seen that this was a violation of the terms of the Union or for reasons of expediency, Queen Anne discontinued the session of parliament in April before the restrictions could be put in place (MacInnes 2007, pp. 308–309). The mercantilist striving of both sides however was still clearly on display.

It is curious that the amount of £300,000 entered the conversation again. However, it is even more curious how adamant the English Parliament was that the Scottish commercial entrepreneurs, and thus Scotland as a nation from a mercantilist viewpoint, should not gain in trade from any activity in the four remaining months of its independence. The English Parliamentarians wanted to ensure that England maintained the advantage of trade through May 1. Because of Queen Anne's suspension of the session, it cannot be known what impact the strictures would have had. As a mercantilist policy, however, it is very clear in intent. If the parliament were in favor of free trade between Scotland and England, then there was nothing wrong with what the Scottish merchants attempted to do, but if one must always maintain a positive trade balance and not allow free competition among all merchants, then certainly the prescriptions make sense. The relations between the two countries both before and after the Union were not about advantage in trade alone but advantages in trade and politics that allowed one to limit the gains of others.

6.1 Balance Sheet: Gains, Losses, and Rhetoric

From a positive balance perspective the Union was a means of transferring or transmuting Scotland's capital into England's own through, ostensibly, the creation of a new nation. However, the Union treaty required the alteration or dissolution of Scotland's political and economic institutions according to the dictates of the English commissioners, while England's institutions did not change. In essence the Union can be seen as a bloodless takeover of assets and dissolution of the government of its northern enemy, but it was no less violent or free of loss for all of that.

According to Carruthers and Espeland (1991), the rhetoric of mercantilist balance logic is that it is rational and unbiased. Some of this can be seen in the calculation of the Equivalent, as discussed in Chap. 5. The logic of the Equivalent calculations obscures the political arithmetic at play in the notion of what the payment was supposed to cover. While the calculating committee conferred authority and impartiality by their figures, the contents of the Equivalent and the discussion of its uses in Article XV was biased. The opaque decision-making process to determine the number of Scottish representatives in the new parliament, as well as Defoe's attempt to develop a logical rationale for the lopsided balance of seats discussed in Chap. 4, is another example. More can be seen in the rationale for Scotland to join England in the Union, that it was an underdeveloped country that could neither build its own commercial empire, in part due to English policy that created a situation such that that was the case as seen through the Navigation Acts, the treatment of the Darien colony, and the threatened Alien Act, nor engage in full-scale self-defense, as demonstrated in Chap. 2. In the mercantilist world of Davenant and Mun, these were rational arguments that if put in terms of "number, weight, and measure" as Petty prescribed could be seen as arguments that were based in economic logic rather than political or national biases (Petty 1690, p. 244). But of course, as has been shown, mercantilist rhetoric appeared impartial and bloodless but was used to justify policy that had damaging structural effects through structural violence all the same.

The maneuvering of the Scottish Parliament into a position where they felt they had no choice but to go to war or to treat for Union was itself a form of structural violence. However, these measures did not cease once the commissioners were appointed and agreed to meet. The treatment of the Scottish commissioners and discounting of their ideas for other arrangements that would allow a more equal balance of power in the United Kingdom were just as impactful as physical invasion as far as the future of the Scottish nation was concerned. Extending freedom of trade to the plantations but then imposing strictures on customs, shipbuilding, and demanding the dissolution of the Company of Scotland were economically damaging and intended to dismantle the country's mercantilist power. In the calculation of the Equivalent and the rhetoric surrounding it in Article XV, the public, and perhaps the ministers of parliament, were misled into thinking that a full recompense would be made for a variety of financial losses but that was not the case. Although the dissolution of the Scottish Parliament and movement of the capital city to London was a forceful act, perhaps the most severe structural violence that was crafted into the Act of Union was the composition of the new parliament. The construction of representation in the new parliament ensured that the Scottish ministers would always be outvoted as a group and that the entirety of Scotland would not be as thoroughly represented as it had been in the Scottish Parliament. That the number of seats was based on Cromwell's arbitrary allotment and then justified on the basis of land taxation, ensured this even more so than if the number had been calculated according to population or total taxation alone. The low number of Scottish representatives guaranteed potential structural violence into the future. The shift or elimination of Scotland's political and economic institutions in a manner that favored English mercantilist goals and policies was accomplished through legislation rather than warfare was sought not necessarily to inflict damage on Scotland's economy but on its ability to ever fight back or gain an upper hand, either commercially or politically, under the new status quo. As Fletcher had warned, in a parliament dominated by English ministers, Scottish trade could be controlled through basic legislation or through the corruption of their 45 ministers (Dalrymple 1768, p. 68). These actions, mercantilist in nature, shifted power even more firmly in England's favor, granting a perpetual advantage in parliamentary decisions.

Under a positive-balance or a foreign-paid income view of the world, one must always seek to gain an advantage over one's rivals in any exchange. What then did England gain in exchange for the Union? Previous treatments have focused on the gain of security both in the Protestant succession and in a cessation of enmity between neighbors, and confidence that Scotland would not now make an alliance with France. However, from the perspective of trade, value, and transmutation, England gained all of Scotland's resources, including its people who would return from abroad, merging them with its own, which was the perspective shown in the pamphlets for English audiences cited earlier by Defoe and others. The volume of trade between the two countries would increase and the threat exhibited by Scotland's potential as a trade rival overseas would cease. It gained people for its manufacturing and personnel for its military. Just as important was that the rival for access to financial capital was also eliminated, increasing investment funds available for English trading companies and other ventures. G.P. Insh (1924) shows that the main English investors of a number of joint stock ventures in Scotland, the Company of Scotland, the Bank of Scotland, and the Act for Establishing the Manufacture of Baize, were all the same people, revealing that from 1693 to 1695 there was "a persistent campaign on the part of a group of London financiers to find an outlet for their capital in Scotland" (p. 291). The company's founding occurred at a time when various traders in England attempted to break the monopoly of the East India Company through the establishment of rival firms. However, the East India Company's charter was renewed and its competitors fell by the wayside. The former competitors' investors sought alternate outlets for their funds, some of which had gone to the Scottish enterprises. The elimination of the Company of Scotland ensured that the majority of financial capital in England would continue to flow to the East India Company.

The Scottish ministers who voted for the Union viewed elements of the articles as a bonus for the country. Although they would experience a great loss of political capital and the capital itself, a large motivating factor in their arguments is the potential increased flow of financial and physical capital into the country from increased trade and from English investors. There was opportunity for more financial capital to flow into the country from England and opportunities to invest more in trade to the plantations. From a mercantilist perspective, this access to wider trade was the essential element of power and growth and thus was a major factor that carried the Union vote in the Scottish Parliament. On a personal level, many of course also received payments from the Equivalent and for their services as ministers, but many of these were more reimbursements for service than bribes. However, a factor that likely had great persuasive power was a negotiated amendment to Article XXII on the number of representatives. In return for such a low number of representatives, the English agreed that all current Scottish peers, not just the 16 who would be in the new parliament, would have the same rights as English peers. One of the most influential was protection from debtors' prison, which was a privilege that did not previously exist in Scotland (Scott 1994, p. 3773).

Investigating certain elements of the Articles of Union one can see the influence of the power balance theory of Davenant and the influence of political arithmetic, the use of figures and logic in order to attain certain political ends. For instance, although it made sense for the English to maintain dominance in the united parliament due to reasons of population and tax contributions, what was the reason to not allow more Scottish representation? The only answer of the English commissioners was that they were being asked to do too much if they had to alter their parliamentary structure, and alter party membership by allowing more Scottish ministers to sit. By their own admission, their own representation was not fully based on taxation (Clerk 1993, pp. 86–87). There was no reason for this or the scaling up from the Cromwellian distribution on the basis of taxation to be the basic metric except for mercantilist thinking that saw a means to predetermine England's long-term legislative advantage.

It is important to note that mercantilism itself would not see it as unjust that England sought to maintain its political power in the new relationship. The number of Scottish representatives in the new parliament was based somewhat on the proportions of taxation which were themselves based on land rather than jurisdiction. Therefore, representation for the Scottish ministers in the new parliament was based not on territory, population, or heritable jurisdictions but on value. Why should the Scots use their customs and excise revenue to finance English debt instead of keeping their funds for their own debt in the first place? Rather than it being just because that is what the English did and the actions of both nations had to be uniform, the answer was that it was due to the flows of financial capital that made this arrangement convenient for the payment of the English debt. These decisions were not immutable but were deliberate choices that were structurally violent whether those who proposed them and those who voted for them were aware of it or not.

6.2 After the Union: Capital and the Capital

A major physical transmutation that was a requirement of the Union was the movement of the seat of government from Edinburgh to London. Transformation was required of Scotland's other political institutions as well, in the dissolution of the parliament, the changes to the legal system where it needed to be consistent with English law, and in its economic institutions as per the articles. Changes in both continued beyond May 1, 1707.

While the Act of Union established that development of the fisheries and manufacturing would take place, it did not establish that it was the Scottish who would direct this development. "Vast Numbers of Surveyers, Collectors, Waiters, and in short, all or most of the Officers of the Customs and Excise were sent down from England," Lockhart reports. Most of the agents sent not only treated the Scottish poorly, but were also formerly convicted criminals whose motivation was profit rather than development (p. 342). The Scottish Privy Council was dissolved in 1708 and was not given a part to play in the administration of Scotland's affairs. Discontent grew among the population and 1708 also saw the first Jacobite uprising. A measure in 1713 in the new parliament in London to dissolve the Union failed to pass by a mere four votes, indicating a degree of English displeasure as well. Other challenges to the Union followed in 1714, an attempt to legally dissolve the Act on the death of Queen Anne, and the first major Jacobite uprising in 1715, rendering Hamilton's words about the Union creating rebels out of loyal subjects somewhat prophetic.

The hoped-for Scottish economic improvement did not occur swiftly or evenly after the Union. Because of the removal of the capital to London and the consolidation of administration, many middle-class government and military administrators became unemployed. The hoped-for economic improvement did not appear evenly or swiftly (Fry 1998, p. 47). The old parliament courts in Edinburgh were turned into law courts. Glasgow seemed to be the only beneficiary of the open markets and many domestic producers suffered from the influx of less-expensive English goods (Pittock 2001, pp. 64–65). The wool and cattle trades benefited from the extension of the market, but these caused their own disruption as pasturage became more profitable than agriculture and landlords cleared tenants in order to raise more livestock (Smout 1983). T.C. Smout (1963) shows that substantial economic improvement for the country did not begin until the 1730s. Even Defoe, who had claimed that free trade would bring accelerated growth for Scotland, confessed, "that this is not the case, but rather the contrary" when he made his tour of Britain 20 years after the Union (1727, p. 33).

The consolidation of power in London, coupled with the fact that the English had not had to change their institutions brought with it several dangers. One was the danger that Andrew Fletcher and other civic humanists had pointed to of having a major city as the main seat of power, which drew not only political power and corruption to itself but also the trade of the rest of the country, both in terms of physical and financial capital. In Davenant's assessment, these were the roles of the seat of an empire. There is a cognizance in both contemporary mercantilist and civic humanist literature, represented here by Davenant and Fletcher, respectively, of the importance of both capital resources and *the* capital. Certainly, a nation's capital is important from a cultural and traditional perspective and for governance. However, there is also discussion in seventeenth- and eighteenth-century England and Scotland about the dangers and characteristics of republics, commercial empires, and a universal monarchy, as it was feared France could potentially obtain. In his political writing, Fletcher cautions against the ills to a weaker kingdom being absorbed into a union by a stronger kingdom. The capital city is never based in the weaker country and thus the stronger country will always draws resources away to its capital city. Davenant openly concedes that the central city of a trading nation is the vital foundation of an empire and riches will flow to the capital to expand empire:

> Where the seat of dominium is in a great emporium, … such a city will not only be the head of power but of Trade, governing all its branches, and giving the rules and price; so that all parts thereon depending, can deal but subordinately to it, til at last it is found that provinces work but to enrich the superior kingdom. (1699, p. 102)

The very things that Davenant lauds are those that Fletcher fears, in particular that if Scotland becomes a mere province of the British Empire, it will always enrich England and become a dependent nation. Additionally, not only would all trade flow to London but so too would all laws regarding trade flow from London.

It should also be noted that there is another connection with abstraction and distance, discussed in Chap. 1, which is found in Davenant's conception of England's empire. It is no longer to be an empire gained by armies or navies going out and conquering new land with invading forces. When forces are used, they are to safeguard the trade that has been established. The empire extends its lines of trade and its lines of credit rather than platoons of soldiers. Although Davenant makes a distinction between empires for expansion and empires for trade, it is a distinction with very little difference. Both are based upon the notion of expansion and of "superior" kingdoms taking actions to purposefully hinder the trade expansion of other kingdoms or provinces to the point of dependence on the dominant kingdom. This too is conquest and expansion simply through different means than those used in the past. Davenant's theory both justifies and is utilized by the English government.

Fletcher made the case based on Davenant's arguments in the treaty debates that Scotland would never have agency over its affairs again if it joined the Union. The danger of removing the capital from Edinburgh, because it signaled that Scotland was seen as a dependent nation, was that it would always be kept such in the internal balance of power in the new central government. At the same time, the English government would have eased due the location of the capital in London and also draw a greater amount of economic activity toward itself, to the detriment and drainage of financial and physical capital from the rest of the country. As Fletcher argued in his 1706 pamphlet against incorporating Union, unless Scotland were given more political authority over its own affairs, a joint government centered in London would always put England's interests first. He recognized the mercantilist principles at play.

6.3 Gains from Political Trade

Despite the imbalance of gains and the structural violence that was inherent in the Articles of Union, both countries gained positive benefits from the Union. What then was the gain, or the positive balance, in the political trade for those who supported the Union? As stated at the outset, the

Union was not contracted between a set of all-powerful English ministers and powerless Scottish ones. The Scottish ministers who voted for the Union had logical reasons for doing so in the mercantilist framework. One obvious gain was access to trade. Additional gains were political but had no less economic implications. John Robertson (1995) describes the views of the pro side as seeing the incorporating union in Grotian terms as a communication of rights, granting the Scots the security of liberty and property that the English already enjoyed. These and the access to trade would encourage more manufacturing and commerce overall. It can be argued that they examined the gains in terms not of independence and sovereignty, but of agency and what the Union allowed people to do. The Union from this perspective allowed a way out from the limitations of power that had been exerted on Scottish economic action in the years previous to 1707.

However, perhaps counterintuitively, rather than pursuing colonial trade as a sovereign country, the Union promoted the growth and development of Scotland through domestic improvements in manufacturing and enterprise (MacInnes 2007, p. 325). Although individual Scots would benefit from the field of opportunities now available overseas, the engine of growth at home would be through growth of manufactures. Scotland would transmute from a struggling colonial pretender to a sub-territory of a greater empire that had all of the successful mercantilist characteristics of positive balance of trade, colonies, and ability to provide for its own self-defense. The English had exerted their power through mercantilist means to limit the economic actions of the country. Joining the economic empire of England in Great Britain caused a loss of political and colonial power but for those in favor of Union, they saw that it expanded the field of economic opportunities and capabilities, to use Amartya Sen's (1999) phrase, that the Scots could enjoy.

The stability and expansion of locations in which the Scottish people could exercise economic agency that joining the empire made possible also allowed the emergence of a new discourse counter to mercantilism. There is a strong sense in which Scottish political economy and the Scottish Enlightenment can be seen both as made possible because of the Union and as reactions to the Union.

6.4 Human Capital

Although it would seem that Scotland lost much of its social capital in the form of the leadership who had to move to London and those who simply lost their positions through the consolidation of the court and parliament and also saw a movement of persons to England thereby, Scotland still had another ample source from which to draw upon for its development: the education of the middle and upper classes and the impulse for improvement across society. What then replaced the old institutions of Scotland after the Union? It is salient to note that part of the Articles of Union safeguarded the institutions of the Presbyterian Kirk and the Scottish legal and university systems. Leadership and social capital were still generated from each.

Despite the dissolution of the independent state, Scottish institutions ensured the survival and ongoing positive transformation of Scottish society. As I have argued elsewhere, economic concerns became one of the spaces in which, in the absence of a traditional political state, the Scottish could exercise their agency (Ramos and Mirowski 2011). One example of this not explored in the previous document is in the variety of improving societies that formed that focused not only on the advancement of the economy but also on educational pursuits. The economic emphasis of these societies and their intended contributions are notable. The Society of Improvers in the Knowledge of Agriculture was established in 1720 and lasted through the 1740s, its reins taken up by the Select Society in 1754 (Livesey 2009, p. 19). The improvement societies all engaged in economic development. Literacy, engagement with civil and economic issues, improved infrastructure, and an improved food supply are all hallmarks of economic development programs even today. An advancement of both physical and human capital allows for societies to reach the higher rungs of the development ladder as explained by modern development economists, such as Joseph Stiglitz (2002).

Education at the local level was also an important factor in building Scotland's human capital. The Scottish Kirk was a source of the development of Scotland's "intellectual capital" from the seventeenth century onward. An act passed in 1633 ensured that any person who would hold an office or any form of leadership in Scotland would have access to education, and thus the robust grammar school system in Scotland was born. With its focus on leadership from the local level, the family, and the local community, the system encouraged independent thought. Every town in the large burghs of Scotland had its own grammar school (Saville 2008; Emerson 1995). The number of subjects taught at the schools increased in the 1720s to include mathematics, navigation, geography, and accounting (Withrington 1970, p. 170). All of these subjects were of great use to a nation hoping to engage not only in more international trade but also in domestic improvements and commercial growth. The reform of the university system and further development of the Scottish legal profession in also contributed to the intellectual approach to all stages of life and a sense of the interconnectedness of the parts of society.[1]

The continued development of human and social capital laid the foundation of human capital that was able to create the Scottish Enlightenment and the science of political economy, which itself makes use of an intellectual approach based on interdependence to answer the question of how societies, and the state in which the people reside, provide for their material wants. In the work of Sir James Steuart (1767), grandson of the Lord Advocate Steuart and also educated in the law, the first to publish an English-language treatise on economics as a subject, and his successor Adam Smith (1776), a product of the Scottish university system, one finds a very different theory of economic activity and policy than that which created the Union. After all it is Smith who wishes to dispel the belief in the positive balance concept when he writes in the *Wealth of Nations* that:

> Nothing, however, can be more absurd than this whole doctrine of the balance of trade, upon which, not only these restraints … almost all the other regulations of commerce are founded. When two places trade with one another, this doctrine supposes that, if the balance be even, neither of them either loses or gains; but if it leans in any degree to one side, that one of them loses and the other gains in proportion to its declension from the exact equilibrium. Both suppositions are false. (IV.3.31)

Note

1. The development and importance of the university system, the legal profession, and other cultural factors are explored in more depth in Ramos and Mirowski (2011), Emerson (1995), Allan (1993), and Clive (1970). An exploration of the religious aspect of the Union debates and the role of the Kirk in Scottish society is in Stephen (2007).

References

Allan, D. 1993. *Virtue, Learning, and the Scottish Enlightenment*. Edinburgh: Edinburgh University Press.

Carruthers, B.G., and W. Espeland. 1991. Accounting for Rationality: Double-Entry Bookkeeping and the Rhetoric of Economic Rationality. *American Journal of Sociology* 97 (1): 31–69.

Clerk, J. 1993. *History of the Union of Scotland and England*, trans. and ed. D. Duncan. Edinburgh: The Scottish History Society.

Clive, J. 1970. *The Social Background of the Scottish Renaissance*, eds. R. Mitchison and N. Phillipson. Edinburgh: Edinburgh University Press, pp. 225–244.

Dalrymple, J. 1768. *Memoir of Great Britain and Ireland*. London: T. Cadell and W. Strahan.

Davenant, C. 1699. *An Essay on the Probable Methods of Making the People Gainers in the Balance of Trade*. London: James Knapton.

Defoe, D. 1727. *A Tour Through the Whole Island of Great Britain*. Dublin: James Williams, 1779.

———. 1799. *The History of the Union Between England and Scotland*. Dublin: John Exshaw.

Emerson, R. 1995. Scottish Cultural Change 1660–1710 and the Union. In *A Union for Empire*, ed. J. Robertson, 121–145. Cambridge: Cambridge University Press.

Fletcher, A. 1706. *State of the Controversy Betwixt United and Separate Parliaments*. Edinburgh.

Fry, M. 1998. Politics. In *Modern Scottish History: 1707 to the Present*, ed. C. Whately, 43–62. East Linton: Tuckwell Press.

Insh, G.P. 1924. The Founding of the Company of Scotland Trading to Africa and the Indies. *Scottish Historical Review* 21 (84): 288–295.

Livesey, J. 2009. *Civil Society and Empire: Ireland and Scotland in the Eighteenth-Century Atlantic World*. New Haven: Yale University Press.

Lockhart, G. 1714. *Memoirs Concerning the Affairs of Scotland from Queen Anne's Accession to the Throne to the Commencement of the Union*. London: Booksellers of London and Westminster.
MacInnes, A. 2007. *Union and Empire: The Making of the United Kingdom in 1707*. Cambridge: Cambridge University Press.
Petty, W. 1690. Political Arithmetick. In *Economic Writings of William Petty*, ed. C. Hull, 232–313. London: Cambridge University Press.
Pittock, M. 2001. *Scottish Nationality*. New York: Palgrave.
Pocock, J.G.A. 1975. *The Machiavellian Moment*. Princeton: Princeton University Press.
Ramos, A., and P. Mirowski. 2011. A Universal Scotland of the Mind. *POROI: An Interdisciplinary Journal of Rhetorical Analysis and Invention* 7 (1): article 3, 42. https://doi.org/10.13008/2151-2957.1077.
Robertson, J. 1995. The Union Debate in Scotland, 1603–1707. In *A Union for Empire*, ed. J. Robertson, 198–227. Cambridge: Cambridge University Press.
Saville, R. 2008. Intellectual Capital in Pre-1707 Scotland. *The Scottish Historical Review* LXXXVII (Supplement): 45–60.
Scott, P.H. 1994. *Andrew Fletcher and the Act of Union*. Edinburgh: The Saltire Society.
Sen, A. 1999. *Development as Freedom*. Oxford: Oxford University Press.
Smout, T.C. 1963. *Scottish Trade on the Eve of the Union*. Edinburgh: Oliver and Boyd.
———. 1983. Where Had the Scottish Economy Got to by the Third Quarter of the Eighteenth Century. In *Wealth and Virtue*, ed. I. Hont and W. Ignatieff, 45–72. Cambridge: Cambridge University Press.
Smith, A. 1776. *An Inquiry into the Nature and Causes of the Wealth of Nations*. London: W. Strahan and T. Cadell.
Stephen, J. 2007. *Scottish Presbyterians and the Act of Union of 1707*. Edinburgh: Edinburgh University Press.
Steuart, J. 1767. *An Inquiry into the Principles of Political Economy*. London: A. Millar and T. Cadell.
Stiglitz, J. 2002. Participation and Development: Perspectives from the Comprehensive Development Program. *Review of Development Economics* 6 (2): 163–182.
Withrington, D. 1970. Education and Society. In *Scotland in the Age of Improvement*, ed. R. Mitchison and N. Phillipson, 169–199. Edinburgh: Edinburgh University Press, 2004.

7

Unintended Consequences: Scottish Political Economy as a Reaction to Mercantilism

Abstract This chapter asserts that the vacuum left by the departure of the Scottish Parliament allowed Scotland's other institutions to continue to develop, which helped to lay the groundwork for the emergence of the Scottish Enlightenment. Scotland's changed economic circumstances and governance post-Union necessitated the emergence of Scottish political economy. The work of Sir James Steuart and Adam Smith is explored as a reaction against the worldview of mercantilism on growth, trade, poverty, and independence. Each author's growth theory demonstrates a growth theory based on interdependence among individuals in society rather than the competition and dependence of nation-states. Rather than interference, the role of government is reassigned as one that supports commerce in the case of Smith and prevents crises in Steuart.

Keywords Mercantilism • Political economy • Adam Smith • Sir James Steuart • Scottish Enlightenment • Trade • Growth • Poverty • Interdependence • Development • Government • Governance

A. Ramos, *Shifting Capital*, Palgrave Studies in the History of Economic Thought,
https://doi.org/10.1007/978-3-319-96403-4_7

The Union made the Scottish Enlightenment probable. The mercantilist economic arrangements and power structure that oversaw the policies of the Scottish economy were determined at a distance in London. Mercantilist themes of positive balances from interactions and zero-sum views of limited prosperity did not coincide well with the relative stability enjoyed in Scotland post-45 and the increase in economic growth and development that began to appear in the 1750s and 1760s. A new vision of economic interaction for commercial society, as opposed to commercial empire, was necessary. The vision included multiple aspects that were a response to mercantilism and to the Union. Reliance on the local rather than on a distant seat of government and a focus on the contributions of the members of economic society rather than the machinations of government ministers and merchants companies was a consistent part of that new vision.

There are multiple factors that contributed to the development of the Scottish Enlightenment and political economy's place within it. Here I wish to situate Scottish political economy as a reaction to, and a transformation of, the rhetoric of mercantilism. Although discourses challenging the tenets and policies of mercantilism emerged in the second half of the eighteenth century, as one can see from Adam Smith's commentary on policy in the *Wealth of Nations*,[1] mercantilist policy was still very much in effect in Britain and elsewhere. Therefore, there was still much to not only write against but also reasons to offer an alternative consistent with the current economic conditions.[2] As Scotland's economy improved, the rise of commerce contributed to different thinking about economic activity. However, at the same time the persistence of trade restrictions and the history of mercantilism required a new way of thinking about production, consumption, exchange relationships, and the role of society in relation to national power.

What I wish to explore is how the focus of Scottish political economy, as represented in the works of Sir James Steuart and Adam Smith, on wealth and policy is different from that of mercantilism.[3] The rhetoric of economic thought begins to change in Scotland due to the results of the mercantilist policies that had been pursued through the Act of Union and the mercantilist processes and mindset that brought the treaty into being. For the authors of the new discourse, power does not reside in an accumulation of state power but in the expansion of the capabilities of individuals in society. The means to attain such power is not in force and destructive competition but in interdependence. Rather than a struggle of all against all, Steuart and Smith create theories of economic activity in which all can be made better off, both at home and abroad. These themes are consistently demonstrated in Steuart's and Smith's growth theory and their treatments of wages and wealth. From this it can be seen that they establish how to gain economic independence, regardless of one's political situation.

7.1 Theories of Growth, Wages, and Wellbeing

What the improving societies of the early eighteenth century that were mentioned in Chap. 6 have in common with the political economy developed by Steuart and Smith is that they focus on economic development rather than economic growth alone and that they rely on changes being made that, in Steuart's case, focus on the importance of the local and administrators' understanding the history and culture of a people, and in Smith's case on private individual and community actions of persons in society to bring about positive economic change. They both focus on the contributions of labor to the wealth of the nation, rather than the influence of government, monopoly corporations, or international trade wars. Each author's growth theory can be read as responses to mercantilism, not only in their providing a new vocabulary by which Scotland could define itself as part of a civil, commercial society rather than a subsumed nation in Great Britain, but also a means of bringing about its own economic improvement that did not necessarily rely on the policies generated in London. In essence political economy both helped to redefine the nation and to deliver a form of self-governance back to the local community.

7.1.1 Circulation and the Surplus: Theories of Growth

Scottish political economy is unique compared to the writings of, say, Mun or Davenant in that it stresses improved quality of life rather than economic growth alone. Steuart says the object of the science of political economy is

> to secure a certain fund of subsistence for all the inhabitants, to obviate every circumstance which may render it precarious; to provide everything necessary for the wants of society, and to employ the inhabitants (supposing them to be free men) … to make their several interests lead them to supply one another with their reciprocal wants. (I, introduction, p. 27)

As he makes clear in the preface, he does not mean that the government is to do this but that a functioning economy should provide these things. Smith uses a very similar definition with the caveat that people do these things for themselves (IV.i.1). In the WN he seeks to uncover the causes of how to best produce "the necessaries and conveniences of life," or the production of basics and luxuries. The basis of the discussion in both Steuart and Smith is different than that of mercantilism as the focus is not on the accumulation of wealth for the state or the commercial conquest of others but of making sure those at home are well provided. Thus, the concept of a surplus continues to be important, but rather than a trade surplus it is a surplus of goods to be used for home consumption in Steuart and for consumption and further production in Smith.

Steuart's *Principles of Political Economy* was published in 1767 and was the first English-language work on economics as a subject separate from politics. The focus on provision is intentional on Steuart's part in his choosing of the phrase "political economy" to name the new science.[4] Oeconomy, from the Greek *oikonomos*, refers to household management, and Steuart says that in the political economy it is the same except the household is the state. As in the Greek study of household management however, the emphasis is making sure all are well off, and thus the focus is on the quality of life of those in the state, or whatever community is under investigation, rather than the positive balance of trade or balances of power.

Steuart's theory of economic development occurs in several stages. Initially in the agricultural stage the economic problem is to generate a stable food supply, and then one whose growth rate matches that of the growth rate of the population. In this stage landlords and farmers make up the two economic classes of society. When productivity produces a food surplus, a new group of persons emerge called the freehands, those who are able to leave agriculture and produce other goods. The rise of the freehands ushers in the commercial stage of society. The three economic sectors begin to exchange goods and payments among each other (I.5–6, pp. 31–59).[5]

With stability in the food supply established, it is "the free hands, by return of their own ingenuity" that cause further economic growth (I.6, p. 33). While such ingenuity could come from any class, and he discusses the innovations landlords should make on their lands and the improvements that farmers can make in their methods, the largest impetus for overall growth of production and exchange comes from the freehands: those who are producing new goods for society and purchasing them from each other. The creation of these new crafted goods and sale of them to landlords and farmers generates income with which the freehands pay rent to the landlords and purchase food from the farmers. From these payments the landlords purchase goods from the freehands and extra food from the farmers. Likewise, the farmers, after paying their rent to their landlords, purchase goods and services from the freehands and occasionally additional or differentiated food from each other (I.6, pp. 33–34). In essence Steuart's social division of labor describes a modern circular flow process of the exchange of goods and services and payments.

Steuart does not see the triad as a hierarchy. No sector is higher than the others in terms of economic stability and each contributes to the wellbeing of the economic state. However growth in the economy depends on new goods created by the freehands and the response of the other sectors. If the freehands either stop making new goods or stop being paid for them, the circular flow of payments and goods and services in the economy breaks down, causing unemployment and disruption of the economic circuit. Just as it can be made smaller by the lack of ingenuity by the freehands or a breakdown in payments, the wheel of commerce can be enlarged or made smaller through the creativity and innovation of the freehands.

Although his main focus is on the material contributions of the freehands to the growth of the wheel of exchange, Steuart also makes clear that increases in population, another booster to the size of the economy, are dependent on the activity of the freehands. Without the incentive to produce a surplus in order to have the new goods the freehands produce, a larger food supply and incomes to sustain increases in family size will not occur. It is possible to maintain a very simple economy without the gifts of the freehands but its growth will be limited if not entirely unsustainable. Steuart says, "Agriculture among a free people will augment population, in proportion only as the necessitous are put in a situation to purchase subsistence with their labour" (I.5, p. 28). Likewise, there will be no growth in population if there is not a means for people to buy agricultural goods because there will be no incentive to create a surplus. Similarly, once expansion to a more diverse economy occurs, if the other sectors lack the sufficient means by which to purchase goods from the other sectors, there will be no economic growth.[6]

Steuart's system is maintained by both the desire of the freehands to better themselves and the incentives every sector of economic society has to continue to participate in the commercial exchange process. Farmers and the landlords both want the luxuries and other goods produced by the freehands and thus demand will increase with the innovation of the freehands, and the freehands' income thereby. Likewise, this situation benefits the landlords and the farmers as the freehands will have more income to spend on the farmers' produce and the landowners' rent. With more disposable income available in society, landowners can capture a portion of it by undertaking improvements on their land and thus charge higher rents. The improvements benefit the agricultural sector, making farmers more productive and increase their incomes by having more and more quality product to sell. Everyone thus has an incentive to participate in the circular flow of goods and payments and to take actions that improve the goods and services for sale in order to increase their own incomes. Although most of Steuart's introductory thoughts on the economic problem center on biology and altruism in that people will naturally follow their desires to procreate and have children and then to provide for their families (I.3, p. 19), self-interest in terms of taking action to better one's quality of life is the driving force in the economic development of society past the initial division into three sectors, and it is the freehands who lead the way (II.1, p. 162).

Trade is vital to keep society functioning but the focus in Steuart's growth theory is not on the production of goods for export, but on the production of goods such that provision is assured and incentives are in place such that the other sectors maintain the balance of exchange. The goal is not necessarily to gain an advantage over the sectors one is trading with but to better oneself. While Steuart does focus on a balance, it is rather the balance of wealth than the balance of trade. The ingenuity of the workers to create new goods and the desires of each sector for the goods of each will, he says, fluctuate over time with what is being offered by each sector. Commercial exchange however is a way in which the balance of wealth is shifted. Landlords will increase the incomes of the freehands by purchasing their wares. The freehands and landlords boost the incomes of the farmers by buying more of the products of agriculture, and both of these sectors will pay higher rents as they demand more or better land. The movement of payments and goods is ongoing and dynamic. Rather than a double-entry view of exchange, Steuart focuses on a circular flow of goods and payments. Steuart extends this same logic to international trade, seeing each nation as a part of an economic division of labor and that wealth will circulate among countries in a fluctuating manner over time as well. While it is essential in Steuart's theory to produce a surplus of goods, it is a surplus that is both for home consumption and to engage in trade overseas. He expands this analysis to fulfilling others' reciprocal wants to international trade beginning (II.1, p. 170). The purpose is to create goods that people want and generate a better standard of living at home rather than the political purpose to maintain a positive balance of trade against one's enemies.

Smith's theory of growth and development is more precise and centers on his theory of capital. The essential elements for growth are the division of labor, described at the micro level in Book I of the WN as opposed to Steuart's more macro approach, and a growing capital stock in Book II. Although the division of labor is important, the more vital aspect of commercial society is the generation of capital: "The great wheel of circulation is altogether different from the goods which are circulated by means of it. The revenue of the society consists altogether in those goods, and not in the wheel which circulates them" (WN II.2.14).

Smith's definition of capital is much more expansive than the modern neoclassical definition of durable goods used in the course of production. The capital stock consists of two major categories: capital used for immediate consumption by the entire nation and capital used to generate revenue for the entire nation. Any food one eats, clothes one wears, and shelter one uses while producing or consuming are capital used for immediate consumption. The stock of goods that is produced in order to be sold, rather than to be consumed by the producer, is in the category of "used to generate revenue." Within this category are two subcategories of fixed and circulating capital. Fixed capital includes objects such as "useful machines," "profitable buildings," "improvements upon land," and "the acquired and useful abilities of all the inhabitants or members of the society" (II.1.23–25). Circulating capital is that which "affords a revenue only by circulating or changing masters." It includes the stock of stock of provisions to be sold (food and drink); inputs that are being made into goods to be sold; finished goods; and the money needed for "circulating and distributing them [the finished goods] to customers" (II.1.11–27).

Who circulates this capital and produces the goods? The various occupations mentioned by Smith throughout the WN as performing this kind of work are brewers, butchers, bakers, weavers, shoemakers, smiths, cabinetmakers, jewelers, goldsmiths, china merchants, shopkeepers, and other manufacturers. These are representative of middle-class occupations in eighteenth-century Britain, which are responsible for creating and circulating capital. The stock used by all for immediate consumption however also needs to be replenished, all the time. Smith identifies the source of the replenishment of this passing capital as "the land, mines, and fisheries." The work of those who engage in hard labor on land, in mines, and in the rivers and oceans therefore also contributes to capital (II.1.27–30).

National wealth is created by the average person living in society, who pursues exchange out of self-interest to have a better life. Although this process is facilitated by merchants and requires the government to create public goods that aid commerce, such as bridges, ports, roads, and education, as discussed in Book V of the WN, it is not driven by monopoly agreements between the two. Average people carrying out their daily business allocate their resources as they see fit in the course of their daily lives, both creating and circulating the capital stock that is the basis of the national standard of living. Rather than the focus on fierce commercial competition between nation-states, Smith and Steuart show that wealth is generated through a combination of self-interested desire for self-improvement for oneself and one's family and interdependence. In Steuart, the three economic sectors all support each other, just as in Smith the creation of new capital depends upon the circulation of capital, and of each person playing one's part in the division of labor.

The growth theories presented here are a departure from mercantilism both in their goals of wellbeing across society and in the means by which this is attained. It is not a trade surplus carried by merchants that causes a nation to attain wealth and power but a surplus of, first, food and then other goods and the resources to make those goods being circulated in the economy that produces strength and stability. Power is to be found in provision, improvement, and incentivizing profit and wages. While an accumulation of capital is similarly important in both, in the treatment of Scottish political economy capital is multifaceted and is created by industriousness rather than by absorption, transmutation, or conquest.

7.1.2 Population, Poverty, and Wages

The treatment of population, poverty, and wages is linked to and consistent with the outlook in each author's growth theory. Population is stressed in Steuart not for the sake of having an available workforce for production of goods for export but for the purpose of creating and circulating the wealth of the nation. Smith does not explicitly address the topic of population as earlier writers had but has much the same emphasis as Steuart when it comes to the labor force: Their purpose is to produce and sell goods to improve their own lives and the lives of others. The notion of improvement is the form of self-interest that both authors stress in the end. Although of course the modern discourse of economics tends to focus on greed as the central component of self-interest as a goad to human action, a close reading of the texts of Smith and Steuart shows that they more often discuss self-interest in terms of the betterment of conditions for oneself and one's family.

An important aspect of Scottish school of economic thought is a persistent concern about poverty and improving living standards for the majority of the people, whereas mercantilism's analysis of poverty focuses more on why a nation does not produce enough goods to be a commercial or military threat to other nation-states. Mercantilism's focus on lowered production costs to keep exports competitive did not often advocate a high quality of life for the laborer. Mercantilist theorists advocated a system of subsistence wages for those producing goods for export. The notion that the desire for betterment of one's situation would cause an increase in productivity and, therefore, higher wages was connected to higher amount of capital output. Steuart says the ingenuity of the workers is the wealth of the nation and Smith saw labor as producing the true wealth of the nation. Given this importance of labor, both make the argument that productive work in general, that adds to the capital stock or that increases standards of living, must be compensated above subsistence and in proportion to productivity. However, this is merely a base level of wages, and often needs to be higher than that.

Subsistence wages, what Steuart calls the "physical necessary," are not enough. He asserts that worker compensation should be commensurate with one's station in life, which he calls the political necessary (II.30, p. 495). A lawyer, for instance, needs a wage high enough not only to survive, but to survive with dignity in his field, that is, to afford the robes, wig, and other accouterments necessary to his station. Wages should be equal to a basic amount for both a physical and a political necessity. Smith likewise discusses how wages are based on labor hours but that there are compensating wage differentials for difficulty of work and other matters. However, he also says that a laborer needs to make enough to support himself and his family at a basic level:

> A man must always live by his work, and his wages must at least be sufficient to maintain him. They must even upon most occasions be somewhat more, otherwise it would be impossible for him to bring up a family, and the race of such workmen could not last beyond the first generation. (I.8.15)

This is a radical departure from the population theory and wages theory of mercantilist thought and indeed even early French political economy of the same period, such as in the work of Richard Cantillon (1755) and the physiocrats. Although Wiles shows (1968) that this is certainly not true of all theorists of the period, for Petty and many other mercantilist theorists of this kind subsistence wages were seen as both necessary and immutable as they were assumed to have a direct relationship with population and an inverse one with work effort (Hutchison 1988; Furniss 1920). Higher wages would cause workmen to be able to support more children and thus would cause an increase in family size. The resulting increase in population and eventually in the labor force once those children grew up would cause competition for work and thus cause wages to fall. The fall in wages would have a depressive effect on population and bring the labor force back into balance with the number of jobs available. Rather than an observation of what was actually occurring in labor markets and with wages in the seventeenth and early eighteenth centuries, the subsistence wages theory is more of a justification for the conditions imposed on the working population by policymakers' adherence to mercantilism.

7.2 New Balance

Steuart and Smith each address the pursuit of a positive balance of trade and acknowledge its benefits. Commerce "without force constraint" between two nations would always benefit both, although not equally, Smith wrote (IV.3.31). Trade, he continues, ought to be "a bond of union and friendship between nations," and harshly criticizes "the capricious ambitions of kings and ministers" and "jealousy of merchants and manufacturers" who used it otherwise (IV.3.38). Previous assessments of Steuart as a mercantilist, such as Anderson and Tollison (1984), are misguided in seeing his skepticism regarding free international trade as being rooted in the theories of the seventeenth century.[7] A further reading of Steuart's remarks on international trade show that he opposes a "completely open trade" among countries at different levels of development because of the damage that can be inflicted on the infant industries of weaker countries on the one hand and the profligacy that can be introduced when a developed nation moves away from producing for itself and becomes dependent on other countries' exports to the detriment of its own industry (I.23; II.29). He recognizes the advantages of international trade and of having a trade surplus, but also cautions that the benefits of such can turn against a country's wellbeing (I.5–6). Like Hume he recognizes that a country cannot always maintain a positive trade balance.

However, the balance metaphor did not disappear from Scottish economic discourse but merely changed form. Rather than seeking a positive balance against other countries, the balances pursued by Smith and Steuart are internal. An even balance between population and the food supply is the necessity of Steuart's most basic level of development. A positive balance of food compared to population is what allows the economy to move the next stage, where again a positive balance of manufactured goods is necessary for the three sectors to provide for each others' wants. At the more advanced stage of the commercial economy, the positive balance that the economy must produce is between "work and demand" (employment and the demand for goods) (II.10–11). The positive balance of trade, rather than being the ultimate goal of national economic activity, is relegated to one of many balances, all the others of which are more necessary, whose function is to provide for national provision and quality of life.

Smith likewise acknowledges the folly of pursuing a positive trade balance, especially as the goal of a nation and national policy. It is Smith who spread the reductive notion that mercantilist theory conflated wealth with specie that is carried through the writings of McCullough, into Viner, and still found in works today, as Magnusson describes (1994, pp. 21–38). However, Smith firmly states in the same Book IV what the capital error of mercantilism is: it privileges production above consumption:

> Consumption is the sole end and purpose of all production; and the interest of the producer ought to be attended to only so far as it may be necessary for promoting that of the consumer … But in the mercantile system the interest of the consumer is almost constantly sacrificed to that of the producer; and it seems to consider production, and not consumption, as the ultimate end and object of all industry and commerce. (IV.8.49)

Besides this unnatural situation where production is put above consumption, mercantilism also causes a misallocation of resources. The elaborate structure of trade restrictions moved resources into certain kinds of production to which they might not have flowed in the absence of such trade protection. Consumer demand is to drive what kinds of goods are produced and thus the allocation of resources to their production, but mercantilist policy forces certain kinds of production to take place. These are unlikely to be those that consumers would have chosen on their own, and thus policies that are ostensibly designed to promote national wealth actually thwart it. The ones who benefit are the merchants "whose interest has been so carefully attended to" (IV.8.54).

Rather than attending to merchants' profits, Smith says a more important balance to be attended to is not the positive balance of trade, which causes employment and capital stock to move into particular industries, but the positive balance of capital stock and employment. Earlier in Book IV he explains,

> The general industry of the society never can exceed what the capital of the society can employ. As the number of workmen that can be kept in employment by any particular person must bear a certain proportion to his capital, so the number of those that can be continually employed by all the members of a great society must bear a certain proportion to the whole capital of that society, and never can exceed that proportion. No regulation of commerce can increase the quantity of industry in any society beyond what its capital can maintain. (IV.2.3)

Further, the capital stock itself is dependent on the balance of a country's annual output and consumption, which "necessarily occasions the prosperity or decay of every nation" (IV.3.44). A society that produces more value in its production than it consumes creates more capital by its savings, which will lead to further growth. In the opposite case,

> the capital of the society must annually decay in proportion to this deficiency. The expence of the society in this case exceeds its revenue, and necessarily encroaches upon its capital. Its capital, therefore, must necessarily decay, and together with it the exchangeable value of the annual produce of its industry. (IV.3.44)

Thus, a country could have a negative balance of trade, but as long as the true balance that determines its growth and wellbeing is positive, the country will continue to flourish.

Because it is revenue and expenditure that matter rather than a gain from every transaction, when Smith considers the subject of colonies and dependency from a cost-benefit perspective. This analysis is still related to defense but rather than Davenant's argument regarding self-defense as examined above in Chap. 3, Smith puts the onus on the mother country, not the colony, to consider the costs of the colonial arrangement. If the American colonies, for instance, will not pay taxes when they cost so much to defend, they should be let go rather than for Britain to continue to fight to hold them (V.3.84–89). The mercantilist framework is transformed away from restrictions on trade or purposely disadvantaging others in an exchange, to what affects the long-term accumulation of capital.

What this demonstrates in relation to the discussions of previous chapters is that the vision of a growing commercial society offered by Steuart and Smith is based on basic factors of demand and exchange, both things that are under control at a local level, rather than the actions that other nations may choose to take in relation to one's trade. The field of economic activity is not on the "empire of the seas" but in the day-to-day decisions that take place in numerous households, fields, and workshops across society. Unlike mercantilism where growth is dependent on certain kinds of production, the actions of merchants and merchant companies, and foreign consumers, in Scottish political economy all members of society, intentionally or not, contribute to national growth.

7.3 Governance and Structural Violence

Another contribution of Scottish political economy that is just as relevant today as it was during the Union is of what good governance consists in relation to the economy. While there are also numerous aspects of this topic that can be explored, in keeping with the themes of the present work the focus here will be on Steuart's and Smith's implicit condemnation of structural violence in the form of economic restrictions and corporate favoritism.

Smith makes clear in Book IV that government has allowed itself to be used by the merchants to create policies granting them monopolies not only abroad in the trading companies but also for certain producers at home due to restrictions on importation. Because this is a manipulation of economic activity, a "manipulation of the law," he says, designed to benefit producers rather than consumers, Smith sees this as structural violence, and he opposes it. Steuart has a more cautious approach to the subject, and as ever for him it depends on particular circumstances. Protection of infant industries against the influx of goods from a more developed country, for instance, can benefit the common good. So too he thinks a merchant company can aid the common good if they are the first to explore a new territory and open it to trade. However, he also allows for the fact that these privileges can be manipulated.

Both support the government provision of public goods. In Book V, Smith emphasizes that these are public institutions and works that support commerce, such as infrastructure, national defense, the legal system, but also a system of ongoing adult education. These all aid in either the circulation or the creation of the capital stock. In addition to these activities, Steuart imbues his legislature with the power to encourage economic activity when necessary to avoid crises, and to intervene in times of crisis, such as purchasing excess goods in times of economic downturns, creating employment programs for the poor, and the establishment of public granaries in times of plenty to provide assistance to the public in times of scarcity. Whether these are sound or faulty policies is beside the present point. What they all point to is a kind of structural benevolence rather than structural violence in order to help bolster an economy. As in the basic theory of growth of both economists, the structural benefits are focused on the domestic economy instead of trying to force the actions of other countries.

From Smith's discussion of persuasion and domination in his *Lectures on Jurisprudence* one can argue that structural violence and domination are unnecessary in a commercial society. He says that the tendency to trade and the tendency to dominate are both rooted in a need to persuade others:

> Thus we have shown that different genius is not the foundation of this disposition to barter, which is the cause of the division of labor. The real foundation of it is that principle to persuade which so much prevails in human nature. When any arguments are offered to persuade, it is always expected that they should have their proper effect … We ought then mainly to cultivate the power of persuasion, and indeed we do so without intending it. Since a whole life is spent in the exercise of it, a ready method of bargaining with each other must undoubtedly be obtained. (B.ii.221–222)

Earlier in the *Lectures* he says similarly, "The offering of a shilling … is in reality offering an argument to persuade one to do so and so as it is for his interest" (A.vi.I.56).

Commercial exchange can be a means to overcome the need to dominate, as both are a means of being recognized by others. However, this is difficult because to dominate is to enforce one's will on others, whereas to exchange requires one to engage with the needs of the other. Exchange is a means of overcoming domination. As Lewis argues, one way this is possible is that free commercial exchange creates more wealth than a situation of domination, and another is that exchange broadens the field of possibilities for recognition by others (288). What Lewis overlooks however is that the difficulty can be overcome due to Smith's labor theory of value. Free exchange negates domination because any commercial transaction requires the exchange of equal values of labor hours. In terms of commanding the labor of others, no one dominates in a situation of free commercial exchange because the hours exchanged are the same on both sides. The creation and exchange of goods and services by free nations and individuals thus has the potential to create more wealth than nations and individuals engaged in attempts to dominate, coerce, or manipulate trade with others.

Another relevant commentary on governance by Steuart and Smith concerns the difficulty that arises when government pursues policy that conflicts with the will of the governed. They each recommend a remedy. Steuart also, perhaps unsurprisingly for one who was an active participant in the Jacobite rebellion in 1745, stresses the importance of legislators understanding the "Spirit of the People," which refers to their history and culture.[8] The Spirit of a People may or may not be ready for the best of policies or may not even want or need a well-crafted policy. Policies should be matched as well as possible to a people's Spirit in order for it to be successful and for legislatures to know when the best time to implement a policy is. Given that every community and nation has its own Spirit, Steuart says that there must be different political economies tailored to each one. Although he develops universal principles related to human nature and how economies developed, he did not dictate specific courses of action for every country to follow (I.2). Smith does not have an analogous theory but offers an applicable remedy in the *Theory of Moral Sentiments*. The exercise of sympathy, through the use of the impartial spectator, is a means to overcome divergence of opinion between any two parties in conflict, whether citizens and governors or two nations. However, one has to have the will to use it and it needs to be present on both sides.

7.4 Conclusion

One description of economics is that it is the exercise of adaptation to change (Hayek 1945). The birth of formalized Scottish political economy can be described similarly as an adaptation to the changes that emerged in Scotland after the Union. While the economic thought of mercantilism influenced the politics of the Union, the politics in post-Union Scotland, bolstered by an education system that supported independent inquiry but stressed the fundamental necessity of living in society, in turn influenced economic thought in the development of theories that emphasize not the role of government or merchant monopolies, but of the contributions of local, everyday economic actions to the wealth and wellbeing of the nation. By moving their analysis inward to what contributes at home to domestic wellbeing, a paradigm of exchange was created that was not limited by zero-sum assumptions. Rather than building an empire abroad, the works of Scottish political economy focus on building wellbeing at home and then extending benefits in trade overseas.

The dissolution of the local court and parliament in Scotland, although immediately hurtful, in the long term caused the mercantilist theories of growth and enrichment of the state that relied on government-granted privileges of select firms to seem less relevant than the sources of economic growth close at hand. The removal of the main government apparatus to London allowed for the development of more local economic activity. Smith says the removal of those who were paid by the government caused those who remained to engage in trade and industry to survive, which eventually was more beneficial to the nation (II.3.12). Rather than with a merchant company overseas or government policy, the source of wealth was visible and close at hand. Steuart and Smith saw the source of wealth as average people, from the lower- and middle-income classes, engaged in commercial society together with the landlords. Privileging any one actor in the commercial society stood to disrupt otherwise natural processes.

Smith criticized mercantilist policy for focusing on production for export and its resultant misallocation of capital from what people going about their daily lives would have otherwise used the economy's resources. So too did the Union perhaps misallocate the political and some physical resources of Scotland by moving them into a joint parliament and engaged in joint economic policy, which from the available contemporary sources was different from what the Scottish public may have decided on its own for its own, especially in the matter of its trading partners. Mercantilism's focus is outward, toward conquering others and expansion, rather than through development at home and using the economy as it ought to be used to the Scottish political economists, not as a weapon of war or means of imperial expansion, but as a tool to create an abundance of the "necessaries and conveniences of life."

The mercantilist themes of reliance on the positive balance/zero-sum paradigm, dependency and domination, the use of structural violence, and the use of these to maximize state power were all countered and transmuted into a new worldview in Steuart and Smith. The model of household provision contributed by Steuart and expanded by Smith focuses on a quality standard of living as the metric of national economic strength and independence. Smith's and Steuart's opposition to the favoritism that is displayed in mercantilism is a criticism of the structural violence intrinsic to the system of thought and policy that crafted its proposals to attain a particular outcome to defeat one's rivals. Government, they are both clear, should work for the common good, not to gain an advantage for producers over consumers. Consumers are to be favored because it is domestic demand rather than exports overseas that generates economic stability and growth, and because production exists for consumption. Rather than merchant companies in collusion with government, it is the people in society who generate prosperity by creating and circulating capital, facilitating exchange, and are the source of the real wealth of the nation. The development of the economic thought, found in Steuart and Smith, that stresses interdependence over international domination, and wealth and wellbeing over commercial warfare, was an unintended consequence of mercantilism and the imbalance of outcomes of the Union, and remains one of the Union's enduring positive contributions.

Notes

1. Abbreviated hereafter as WN.
2. Andrew Fletcher's alternative vision presented in the Act of Security explored in Chap. 2 and in his parliament speeches was based more in agrarianism than manufacturing, and so was not necessarily consistent with modern economic conditions. The same is true of the mercantilist colonial growth/trade expansion model Scotland followed previous to Union.
3. I acknowledge David Hume greatly influenced both Steuart and Smith and exclude him here only because he did not produce a formal integrated treatise on economics.
4. The phrase was used previously in French by Monchretien.
5. The page numbers provided refer to the 1767 edition of the *Principles*. The volume and chapter numbers are also provided. For the WN all references are standard, indicating book, chapter, and paragraph.
6. He expands this analysis of fulfilling others' reciprocal wants to international trade beginning in II.1, p. 170.
7. More refutations of Anderson and Tollison that expand beyond my present argument are in Magnusson (1994, pp. 4–7) and Rashid (1986).
8. For a general overview of Steuart's involvement in Jacobitism, see Skinner (1999); and for a more specific discussion of how his Jacobitism influenced his view of the Union and of economics and vice versa, see Ramos (2007), pp. 110–153.

References

Anderson, G., and R. Tollison. 1984. Sir Steuart James Steuart as the Apotheosis of Mercantilism and His Relation to Adam Smith. *Southern Economic Journal* 51 (2): 456–458.

Cantillon, R. 1755. *Essay on the Nature of Commerce in General.* London: Fletcher Gyles.

Furniss, E.S. 1920. *The Position of the Laborer in a System of Nationalism.* Boston: Houghton Mifflin.

Hayek, F. 1945. The Use of Knowledge in Society. *The American Economic Review* 35 (4): 519–530.

Hutchison, T. 1988. *Before Adam Smith: The Emergence of Political Economy 1662–1776.* Oxford: Basil Blackwell.

Lewis, T. 2000. Domination and Exchange: Adam Smith on the Political Consequences of Markets. *Canadian Journal of Political Science* 33 (2): 273–289.

Magnusson, L. 1994. *Mercantilism: The Shaping of an Economic Language.* London: Routledge.

Ramos, A. 2007. *Economy, Empire, and Identity: Rethinking the Origins of Political Economy in Sir James Steuart's Principles of Political Economy*, Doctoral diss. Notre Dame, USA: University of Notre Dame.

Rashid, S. 1986. Smith, Steuart, and Mercantilism: Comment. *Southern Economic Journal* 52 (3): 843–852.

Skinner, A. 1999. Introduction: Sir James Steuart: The Jacobite Connection. In *The Economics of James Steuart*, ed. R. Tortajada, 1–23. London: Routledge.

Smith, A. 1776. *An Inquiry into the Nature and Causes of the Wealth of Nations.* London: W. Strahan and T. Cadell.

———. 1976. *The Theory of Moral Sentiments*, eds. D.D. Raphael and A.L. Macfie. Oxford: Oxford University Press; Glasgow edition. Reprinted, Liberty Press (1982).

———. 1978. *Lectures on Jurisprudence*, eds. R.L. Meek, D.D. Raphael, and P.G. Stein. Oxford: Oxford University Press; Glasgow edition.

Steuart, J. 1767. *An Inquiry into the Principles of Political Economy.* London: A. Millar and T. Cadell.

Wiles, R. 1968. The Theory of Wages in later English Mercantilism. *Economic History Review* 21 (1): 113–126.

Index[1]

A
Abercromby, Patrick, 36
Act Anent Peace and War, 32, 33
Act of Security, 11, 17, 32–39, 70, 71, 78, 137n2
Act of Union, 2, 4, 5, 10, 14, 15, 108, 111, 120
Alien Act, 17n2, 32–39, 62, 68, 90, 107
Allocation, 15, 16, 131
Anne, Queen, 2, 32–34, 38, 51, 62, 69, 77, 105, 106, 111
Armitage, David, 10, 15, 25, 29
Articles of Union, 6, 13, 16, 37, 39n3, 59, 62–81, 97, 109, 113, 115

B
Balance, 6, 9, 11, 14, 16, 17n2, 24, 36, 38, 39, 46, 49, 65, 85, 87, 91, 92, 95, 96, 104–110, 113, 114, 116, 120, 122, 125, 129–132, 136
Balance of trade, 7, 8, 11, 36, 46, 65, 96, 105, 114, 116, 122, 125, 129–132
Balance of wealth, 125
Bank of England, 26, 51
Bank of Scotland, 27, 29, 31, 36, 39n4, 101, 109
Black, David, 36, 38
Black, William, 36, 93, 94
Bowie, Karin, 3

[1] Note: Page numbers followed by 'n' refer to notes.

A. Ramos, *Shifting Capital*, Palgrave Studies in the History of Economic Thought,
https://doi.org/10.1007/978-3-319-96403-4

Brittanic (state formation), 24
Burnet, Gilbert (Bishop), 63, 67, 77, 80

C

Caledonia, 12, 52, 59
Capital, 14–17, 24, 27–31, 45, 51, 55, 58, 59, 62, 71, 78–80, 93, 100, 104–116, 125–128, 130–133, 136, 137
Cato, 9
Chamberlen, Hugh, 38
Clerk, John, of Penicuik, 2, 3, 24, 31, 34, 36, 67, 69–76, 84–86, 92, 95, 96, 98, 104, 110
Colonies, 8–10, 14, 25–31, 48, 50, 53, 55–57, 62, 72, 99, 107, 114, 132
Commonwealth, 25, 47, 54, 76
Company of Scotland, 11, 25–32, 35, 37, 68, 70, 72, 79, 84, 93, 94, 99, 100, 107, 109
Confederation, 64
Council of Trade, 38
Country party, 39n4, 69, 104
Court party, 39n4, 69, 73, 77, 84, 104
Cromartie, George, 36
Cromwell, Oliver, 25, 56, 65, 76, 108

D

Dalrymple, John (Earl of Stair), 28, 72, 75, 108
Darien, 10, 11, 26–31, 36, 39n4, 50, 85, 89, 94, 97–100, 107
Davenant, Charles, 8, 12, 13, 15, 44, 47–52, 54, 55, 66, 107, 109, 112, 113, 122, 132
Debt, 2, 14, 29, 52, 80, 85–89, 92, 94–98, 100, 110
Defense, 16, 44, 48–52, 54, 56, 59, 80, 132
  national defense, 51, 56, 80, 133
Defoe, Daniel, 3, 12, 52, 53, 58, 62, 68, 70, 72, 74, 76, 88, 93, 99, 105, 107, 108, 111
Dependency, 16, 25, 44–59, 132, 136
Dependency theory, 44
Derringer, William, 86, 94, 95, 101
Devine, T. M., 4, 36, 52
Douglas, James (2nd Duke of Queensbury), 34
Dutch, 30, 45, 48, 54, 74

E

East India Company (EIC), 26–28, 37, 46, 79, 93, 100, 109
Edinburgh, 2, 15, 28, 69, 71, 75, 79, 97, 110, 111, 113
Equivalent, 9, 16, 68, 80, 81, 84–101, 105–107, 109
Erskine, John (Mar), 77, 78
Exchange rates, 46

F

Farmer, Paul, 13
Federal union, 11, 17, 25, 44, 67, 71, 73
Finkelstein, Andrea, 9, 50
Fishery/fisheries, 3, 53, 84, 98, 111, 126
Fletcher, Andrew, of Saltoun, 11–13, 17, 18n5, 34, 69, 71, 72, 75, 108, 112, 113, 137n2

France, 9, 32, 34, 36, 56, 66, 86, 90, 108, 112
Free trade, 14, 16, 62, 67, 71, 72, 79, 88, 92, 93, 95, 106, 111

G

Glasgow, 111
Glencoe, Massacre of, 32
Godolphin, Sidney, 37, 49, 62, 63, 66
Goulet, Denis, 9
Grant, Francis, 36
Greg, William, 30, 37
Gregory, David, 85, 86
Growth, 6–11, 15, 17, 25, 29, 32, 33, 36, 45, 47, 48, 53, 57, 96, 109, 111, 114, 116, 120–127, 131–133, 135–137, 137n2

H

Hamilton, James Douglas (Duke of Hamilton), 69, 77, 79, 111
Hanoverian succession, 35, 39n4, 67, 69, 70, 77
Harley, Robert, 30, 37, 105
Hay, John (Marquess of Tweedale), 34
Heckscher, Eli, 7
Highlands, Scottish Highlands, 57, 58
Hont, Istvan, 5, 18n5
Hume, David, 130, 137n3

I

Incorporating union, 24, 35, 37, 44, 62, 67, 68, 113, 114
Independence, independent nation, 17, 44, 48–50, 59, 70, 71, 106, 114, 121, 136
Insh, G. P., 108
Ireland, 10, 16, 25, 28, 32, 48–53, 55–58, 66, 70, 87

J

Jacobites, Jacobitism, 3, 69, 100, 104, 111, 134, 137n8
James VI, 24, 26, 46

K

Keynes, J. M., 6
Kirk of Scotland, 18n4, 59, 115, 117n1

L

Land
  land tax, 64, 74, 76, 108
  and value, 38, 47, 55, 58, 64, 65, 74
Lauderdale (Maitland, John), 25
Law, John, 31, 38, 39n4
Law, Scottish, 29, 39n4, 75, 110
Lenman, Bruce, 36
Lewis, Thomas, 134
Locke, John, 66
Lockhart, George, of Carnwath, 3, 35, 38, 67–72, 74, 77–79, 94, 97, 99, 104, 111
London, 2, 15, 16, 24, 25, 28, 35, 37, 39n4, 53, 71, 72, 74, 75, 78, 80, 93, 96, 105, 107, 109–113, 115, 120, 121, 136

M

Mackenzie, George, 36
MacInnes, Allan, 3, 24, 25, 52, 94, 106, 114

Magnusson, Lars, 7, 8, 48, 130, 137n7
Maitland, John (Lauderdale), 25
Malynes, Gerard, 46
Mar (Erskine, John), 77, 78
McCloskey, Deirdre, 6
McCormick, Ted, 57
Mercantilism, 3–17, 24, 26–31, 44, 46, 62, 99, 110, 114, 120–137
Militia, 3–5, 8, 13–15, 29, 30, 33–36, 50, 51, 57, 58, 68, 90, 97, 108, 111, 128
Mirowski, Philip, 47, 115, 117n1
Misselden, Edward, 46
Molyneux, William, 48, 49
Mun, Thomas, 14, 15, 44–48, 107, 122
Murphy, Antoin, 18n6, 28, 31, 36–38, 39n4

N

Nairne, David, 85
Navigation Acts, 25, 36, 49, 50, 107
Netherlands, 28, 30, 45
Nova Scotia, 25

O

Ogilvy, James (1st Earl of Seafield), 34, 100

P

Pakington, Sir John, 12
Parliament
  English, 12, 16, 25, 27, 28, 30, 33, 34, 37, 49, 71, 75, 104–106
  Scottish, 2, 11, 17, 27, 28, 31–33, 35, 38, 62, 64, 65, 68–77, 84, 85, 94, 107–109
Parliament of Great Britain, 25, 91
Paterson, William, 11, 26, 27, 30, 85, 87
Petty, William, 8, 15, 28, 39n2, 44, 47–49, 52–59, 64, 66, 87, 88, 107, 129
Pittendrigh, J.G., 98, 100
Plantations, 25, 29, 30, 34, 35, 55, 56, 72, 92, 96, 99, 107, 109
Pocock, J.G.A., 47, 52, 55, 104
Political arithmetic, 47, 56, 57, 65, 84–101, 106, 109
Poovey, Mary, 46, 87, 97
Ports, 33, 56, 65, 72, 126
Power, 5–11, 13–16, 24, 26, 30, 31, 33–35, 37–39, 45, 46, 51, 54, 59, 64–66, 68, 71, 72, 75, 76, 80, 90, 93, 104, 107–110, 112–114, 120–122, 127, 133, 134, 136
Privy Council, 111

R

Rashid, Salim, 9, 137n7
Representation, in new parliament, 64, 74, 75, 91, 107–111
Resource allocation, 16, 127, 131
Rhetoric, 5, 6, 10, 12, 15, 65, 87, 100, 106–110, 120
Ridpath, George, 34
Robertson, John, 114
Royal Bank of Scotland, 101
Royal Society, 66

S

Salt, 32, 73, 74
Scotland, 2–4, 6, 8, 10–17, 24–39, 39n4, 44, 46–50, 52, 53, 55–59, 62–65, 67–80, 81n2, 84–101, 104–116, 120, 121, 135, 136, 137n2
Scott, Sir Walter, 66, 109
Scottish Enlightenment, 4, 114, 116, 120
Sen, Amartya, 114
Ships, shipbuilding, 26, 29, 30, 32, 37, 56, 72, 73, 93, 107
Skinner, Andrew, 137n8
Smith, Adam, 7, 11, 17, 116, 120–122, 125–137, 137n3
Smout, T.C., 3, 35, 111
Somers, John (Lord Somers), 8, 18n10, 37, 49, 62–67, 80
Sophia, Electress of Hanover, 32, 71
Southwell, Robert, 66
Spain, 30, 66
Spanish Succession, War of, 32
Spence, C., 86, 97
Squadrone Volante, 39n4, 69
Steuart, Sir James (economist), 17, 116, 120–125, 127–130, 132–137, 137n3, 137n8
Steuart, Sir James (Lord Advocate), 35, 77, 78, 116
Stiglitz, Joseph, 115
Structural violence, 5, 13, 16, 44, 52, 62, 67–79, 84–101, 107, 108, 113, 132–136
Surplus
  agricultural surplus, 123, 124
  surplus of capital, 6, 24, 80
  trade surplus, 9, 47, 51, 122, 127, 130

T

Taxation, taxes, 2, 14, 30, 33, 45, 51, 64, 65, 67, 68, 70, 73, 74, 76–78, 80, 84–89, 92, 93, 95–97, 105, 108, 110, 132
Trade, 2, 4–14, 16, 17n2, 18n10, 24–36, 38, 44–59, 63–66, 70–73, 75, 77, 78, 80, 84, 85, 88, 89, 92, 93, 95–100, 104–109, 111–114, 116, 120–122, 125, 127, 129–136, 137n6
Transmutation, 16, 44–59, 64, 88, 98, 108, 110, 127
Transplantation, transplantees, 56–59
Treaty of Union, 5, 14, 16, 39

U

Union, 2–6, 10–17, 17n2, 18n4, 18n6, 18n10, 24–39, 44–59, 62–81, 84–89, 92–100, 104–116, 117n1, 120, 129, 132, 135–137, 137n2, 137n8

V

Value, theory of, 47, 134
Viner, Jacob, 7, 130

W

Wealth, 7–11, 16, 29, 46, 47, 50, 51, 54–56, 65, 66, 97, 120–122, 125–128, 130, 131, 134–137
Whately, Christopher, 3, 4, 14, 36, 74
William III, 32, 33, 39n4, 51, 62, 69
Worcester(ship), 37
Wylie, Robert, 99

The manufacturer's authorised representative in the EU is Springer Nature Customer Service Centre GmbH, Europaplatz 3, 69115 Heidelberg, Germany. If you have any concerns regarding our products, please contact ProductSafety@springernature.com

Printed and bound by CPI Group (UK) Ltd, Croydon, CR0 4YY
30/09/2026
02225576-0005